Last Dog

And All Those Who Came Before

by

Cynthia Flowers

Last Dog

Cynthia Flowers

COPYRIGHT © 2018 by Cynthia Flowers

All rights reserved. No part of this book may be used or reproduced in any manner whatsoever without written permission of the author except in the case of brief quotations embodied in critical articles or reviews.

Contact Information: Lastdogbook@gmail.com

Cover Art by *Diana Carlile*
Edited by Trish Owens

Published in the United States of America

ACKNOWLEDGEMENTS

I want to thank the extended pack members who supported my husband, Alan, and me in so many ways throughout the eighteen years of joy and sorrow we experienced with all our dogs. This includes family, friends, and those employed to care for them. We could not have done it alone!

Also, a special shout-out to my sister, Claudia, who served as my sounding board, my dear friend Mary Jo who did Yeoman's work editing the first draft of manuscript and my cousin, Joy, who was my Sherpa throughout the publishing journey.

Finally, thank you to those dog behaviorists whose books Alan and I read, and the shows we watched that provided a helpful patchwork of techniques we used to help raise our dogs.

DEDICATION

To Jake, Bailey, Ralf, Charlie, and Abby.
Each of you taught me how to love beyond what I thought I was capable of.

A special thanks...

To my husband, Alan, for giving our dogs what they needed and wanted and making their lives all the richer for it!

PREFACE

My intention in writing this book was to share our real-life experiences of bringing up dogs, starting as first timers, and then eventually transitioning into more seasoned dog guardians, owners, or parents. I leave it up to you to choose the preferred self-descriptor. I know there are a lot of "do-it-yourself" books, classes, and online resources to help navigate this undertaking. But there's something invaluable about sharing a person's—or in this case, a couple's—first-time experiences and lessons learned along the way.

It is my hope that sharing our experiences helps to improve your understanding of your relationship with *your* dog(s). Perhaps, our stories will save you from some of the mistakes we made or avoid some mishaps, thus shortening the learning curve for successful training and disciplining that fosters a more satisfying relationship moving forward.

CHAPTER 1: JAKE

Starting Off on the Wrong Paw

Cynthia with Jake and his pal at Best Friends Animal Sanctuary

To tell you the story about our last dog, Abigail, I need to start with our first dog, Jake, who came to us five dogs and sixteen years ago. Jake started the sequence of events responsible for each and every dog we have had since. It seems like such a long time ago.

We'd been married just two months and my husband Alan, said out of the blue, "Hey, let's get a dog. I've always wanted one."

I don't think there was a full breath between his last word and my first, which was an emphatic, "Yes!"

Alan and I had taken the year off. He'd left his partnership at a broadcast integration company, and I'd left my position as an advertising executive. We both needed a break and a change from not only our work life, but also from where we were living, which was in the New York City metropolitan area. So, we moved from our respective apartments to a town in a then little-known area of the Mid-Hudson Valley in upstate New York, about one hundred miles outside of the city. We rented a house that was perfect for accommodating our two apartment's worth of furniture. With several acres of land surrounded by apple orchards and countless hiking trails in the nearby Shawangunks and Catskill mountains, it seemed like an idyllic setting for us and a dog.

Let me start by admitting that we didn't know very much about dogs when we set out to adopt one. Alan only had cats growing up. On the other hand, I was never successful at convincing my parents to get a dog. All we knew was that we wanted a working or sporting breed, one hardy enough to go on long, mountain hikes and one that liked the water.

So, we decided that a Labrador retriever would be the perfect breed. Other than that, we left caution to the wind and put our trust in an internet search and a single phone call with a breeder.

We made our pick—an eight-month-old, male, black Labrador retriever. Though he seemed a bit on the old side for a puppy adoption from a breeder, we decided to go through with it.

Jake arrived at JFK Airport about a week after our call with the breeder. The poor puppy seemed shell-shocked. He was sitting toward the back of the travel kennel when we crouched down to greet him.

We carried his kennel to the car and put it in the back hatch of our Subaru. We turned down the back seats, so when we opened the carrier inside the car, he had room to come out.

Except…he didn't. This was very odd behavior for a typically gregarious breed. We chalked it up to hours of being stowed in the cargo hull of a plane only to arrive into the arms of strangers.

We had over an hour's drive home. Our excitement grew as we pulled into the driveway. We couldn't wait to let our new friend stretch out his legs and run around a bit.

Luckily, the previous owners of the house had fenced in a small area on this five-acre property as a vegetable garden. It met our needs perfectly for a small dog run, having just enough space.

We pulled the kennel out of the back of the car and gently carried it out to the enclosure. *This is odd,* I thought. *He's still as a stone. Not a peep out of him.* We placed the kennel down inside the yard enclosure and closed the gate.

Despite being on the edge of hopelessness, I told Alan, "I'll open the kennel door while you stand outside the opening to greet our new friend."

After opening the gate, the puppy just stayed inside and didn't even move closer to the kennel opening to sniff the air or take a peek. I was all but ready to give into defeat.

Then Alan blurted, "Some treats—that's what will get him out. Go to the car and grab a few."

However, even the treats failed to inspire Jake to move.

After getting the treats, I suggested, "Let's step outside of the gate and see if that gets him to come out."

Cynthia Flowers

Alan agreed. So we moved out of the enclosure to a spot where we could observe Jake but he wouldn't be able to see us as he came out of the kennel. We waited for what seemed like several minutes. Finally, the tip of his snout emerged to inspect the treats left outside the kennel. Slowly, the rest of him followed.

But something else wasn't right. His posture was crouched down and extremely low, almost crawling as if he didn't want to be seen. Jake was making himself as small as possible. We later learned this was to reduce the risk of being noticed or perceived as a threat.

After a moment or two, Alan and I slowly walked back to the fenced-in area. Jake promptly ran back into the kennel, leaving many of the treats behind. Eventually, he came out again, and I wanted to think it was because he was finally getting used to us.

But he had to pee, and boy, did he pee! When I pulled out the wee pad from his kennel, it was mostly dry to the touch. This poor guy had held it in the entire trip. I suspected he had a urinary tract infection, or UTI for short, so we took him to the vet after that weekend.

"Well," our vet, Karen, said, "he definitely has a UTI, and we can fix that with some antibiotics. However, he does seem to be walking oddly, and it's his hocks that seem to be the trouble. You may want to go see a specialist about his back legs before he gets much older, so you can correct the problem."

I was thinking: *It's not supposed to be this difficult with a new puppy. I expected behavior training, a few accidents in the house, and the occasional chewed on items, but I didn't sign up for this!*

There was a slight pause before she continued, "The other thing that troubles me is his fearful disposition. That may be because he was adopted later than usual after being weaned, especially if he wasn't socialized with people during that time. That could explain his disposition. He may gain confidence as you expose him to more people and other situations."

"It seems like he is always trying to get away from us," I said, confirming her observation. "When I put the lead on him, he frantically pulls in all directions, trying to get away."

Karen gave us the name of someone who specialized in dog behavior and suggested we give her a call.

So we did, and when the behaviorist visited our house about a week later, Jake was wedged between the coffee table and the couch in the living room. Just like when we'd first brought him home, carrying him in the kennel, he didn't make a sound, hoping to go unnoticed. Somehow, we managed to coax him out so the behaviorist could examine him.

After a while, she shook her head. "There's something not right with this dog. It's not only because of his lack of socialization at a young age. There may be something mentally not quite right. He is severely fearful, and you're lucky he is submissive. Otherwise, he'd be dangerous. He could get aggressive, and then you'd have to put him down."

Put him down. That phrase sent a shiver through my body. It was the furthest thing from my mind. *Surely we can help this guy.*

"You could put him on anti-anxiety medication to see if that helps ease him into his new environment and make him receptive to training," she said in response to my reaction.

Cynthia Flowers

We reluctantly took her advice and medicated Jake, but it did not seem to help.

We took him to another person specializing in Labrador retriever training and behavior. She had a program where she'd take in dogs for a boot-camp-style training session. We were hoping that would do the trick. Unfortunately, her energy was all wrong for Jake.

Upon meeting her for the consultation, he pulled away so hard that he snapped open his collar and took off onto a busy main road. I chased him down while waving off oncoming traffic. Luckily, Jake cut to the left down a quiet side street. I don't know how, but I'd had the clarity of mind to pick up his collar and leash when I had set off to get him.

As luck would have it, I found Jake caught in a maze of vine-like bushes. I was able to snap the collar back on and attach the leash and walk—no, actually, drag—Jake back.

When I returned, the woman came to what I thought was an abrupt conclusion. "I can't help him, and I think your only choice is to have him put down."

There was that phrase again, "put down." *Why is everyone so quick to write this guy off?*

Alan and I basically said, "Thanks, but no thanks," and left.

A few days passed with no improvements. Even though we spent as much time as we could with Jake, it seemed to make it worse. When we fed him, we had to leave the kitchen; otherwise, he would not come in to get his food. He had to eat alone.

Putting him on-leash was exhausting, and the walk was even more so. People who passed by during our walks wouldn't say anything, but they would stare or look perplexed because they saw this beautiful, black Labrador pulling away from whoever was walking him and walking ever so oddly in a crouched position with his tail tightly tucked between his two hind legs.

LEARNING: Dog posture is its own language. There is a range of postures, with each conveying a distinct intention or message. Posturing is commonly used among wolves to effectively communicate to other pack members directly or indirectly (i.e., intention). For example, a dog lowers its tail (where glands are located) to possibly minimize its scent so predator or prey have a difficult time detecting them. And in the process, they're alerting other pack members to the type of situation at hand so they also behave appropriately.

A confident dog typically stands with arrow-straight posture with legs wide apart to make itself appear larger than they are, their tail elevated and pointing straight out to make its scent and its presence known. Conversely, a dog that is not confident of its position in the pack and/or the world around them may crouch with its tail tightly tucked between its back legs in an effort to make itself appear smaller than it is and hide its scent.

ALMOST SIX weeks had passed, and it was now Christmas. We were taking Jake on a big outing, a three-hour car ride to my parent's house on Long Island. We were just about ready to leave, carrying out the last of the Christmas gifts to load into the car. Unfortunately, Alan was trying to juggle packages in his left hand while holding the leash in his right.

Cynthia Flowers

On the advice from our vet after the last runaway incident, we'd switched to a choke collar. The vet explained it would give us more control over his pulling. We didn't like the idea of using this style collar, but thought if it could help Jake, then we were willing to give it a try.

The trouble with a choke collar is you need to keep tension on it. If you are too slack, the choke collar becomes loose, and the dog can easily slip out of it. And that is exactly what happened.

In an effort to make sure he didn't drop any packages, Alan dropped the leash to the ground for a second. Just as he was about to put his foot on the leash, Jake must have sensed the relaxed tension. He took off out the front yard and up the road into the apple orchards.

Like before, I went running after him, but of course, he was faster than me. Luckily, our road was infrequently traveled back then and even less so on the holiday, so Jake was spared getting hit by a car.

In shock and feeling distraught, we cancelled our holiday trip to my parents' house that day and to his parents' the next. We felt so responsible for Jake's well-being and guilty that he was in this predicament. We put food out in the backyard, hoping that he would return. We weren't sure if he ever ate what we put out or if the wildlife had enjoyed the kibble. However, we did see Jake later that night in our back yard, but only for an instant.

A few weeks passed, and it was now late January. We'd put out word to the local veterinary offices and dog warden, but he hadn't turned up.

Early one afternoon, I decided to go running. I'm

Last Dog

not sure why I was inspired to do so as it was a very cold day, but the sun was brilliant. Perhaps I needed to work off some anxiety. I started out thinking I wasn't going to do my full route, but the cold dissipated as my body heated up, so I decided to do the full run.

Just as I turned at the midway point in my run, I noticed something out of the corner of my eye, something dark moving in the yard of someone's property. I crossed the road to investigate. As I got closer, I saw it was indeed Jake, crawling into a doghouse.

I had seen this doghouse many times during my runs, long-abandoned like it was just waiting to serve a purpose again. Jake was huddled in the far back end of the doghouse. I was torn about leaving him there, but I didn't have anything to help me secure Jake to bring him home, which was about a mile or so away. I ran back home faster than ever, got in my car, and drove back with leash in hand.

By the time I returned, the property owner's car was in the driveway. I went up to the house and knocked on the front door. A college-age girl answered.

I said, "I'm that dog's owner. His name is Jake, and he ran off some weeks ago. I can't believe I found him. I need to get him into my car. I don't think I need your help, but I'll let you know if I do."

The young girl said, "He's been hanging around our property for a few weeks, just appearing one day out of the woods and making himself at home in the doghouse. We tried to get him into our house, but he would run away whenever we approached. We thought it best to leave food and water in the doghouse where he could stay relatively safe and warm."

Cynthia Flowers

Thank God for people like this. While they were willing to help me retrieve Jake, the doghouse was barely wide enough for one person to even partially insert themselves. I didn't stop to consider how Jake might react as he sat cornered with me reaching in. He could've given me a toothy growl or worse yet, attack.

Instead, he sat motionless and quiet. I grabbed Jake, pulled him out, picked him up, and put him in the back hatch of the car. The leash was not necessary after all. He just let me take him.

I went back to the front porch of the house where the girls were watching.

"I want to thank you so much for giving him food and shelter. Otherwise, I would have never found him," I said, and I was off.

I got him into the house, and like before, Jake couldn't wait to wedge himself between the coffee table and the couch. Although I wasn't surprised, a part of me had hoped he'd behave differently.

Just then, Alan called from the car to say he was on his way back from visiting a friend, and he would be home soon. Obviously, he was unaware of my eventful day. While on the phone, I told him the news. It was initially met with silence. Not the response I was expecting since I was so excited to tell him.

"Where did you find him, and how were you able to get him back home?" he asked.

By the time I finished telling him the story, Alan was pulling into our driveway. When he walked in, he saw Jake in his usual "wedged-in" spot.

Alan said, "In a way, I'm almost sorry you found him. He is going to be so much work, and I don't know how we will be able to keep him."

Last Dog

His disappointment burst my bubble. Up until this point, I had been so happy to have found Jake—elated, actually.

"Isn't it good to know that our mishap didn't cost Jake's life? Also, aren't you amazed that I had spotted him? And for that matter, aren't you impressed that I managed to rescue him on my own?" I was on the defensive. I wondered why he wasn't as happy as I was.

The next morning, I called the vet's office to let them know we had found Jake. Of course, the staff was happy to hear it. One of the vet techs mentioned that there was a woman in Saugerties who specialized in training Labradors, and perhaps we should give her a try. So, we did.

We made a visit to find a household filled with Labradors, and I mean *filled*. They were all related, from the same or subsequent litters. All were lying on top of one of another, cuddling and keeping warm. We stepped back outside to get Jake out of the car.

As soon as the woman set eyes on him, she got an immediate sense of his disposition as he tried to huddle for cover in her outdoor pen. She spent a few minutes observing Jake.

"I am going to let one of my friendliest dogs into the pen with Jake and see how he reacts," Julie said.

As soon as the female Labrador entered, Jake allowed her to approach him without any objection. His posture even straightened. Although he was only cautiously interested, it was an improvement.

"You should consider temporarily taking in another dog as part of Jake's rehabilitation. Sometimes, a dog like this just needs the confidence of another dog to make it feel more comfortable," the behaviorist said.

Alan and I turned to each other with similar shocked expressions that bespoke what we were thinking. *Another dog*? Unfortunately, none of her dogs were offered up, but she did know of a two-year-old female chocolate Labrador that was being fostered by a nearby family.

That weekend, we visited the family—an older couple—and met Bailey. We immediately understood why this couple could not permanently take care of this ninety-five-pound Labrador named Bailey. She had just too much energy. Maybe even for us. There was no other way to describe it; she was a bull in a china shop. This couple was more appropriate for taking care of cats, which they had, or a very old dog.

As if celebrating, Bailey must have run in circles a hundred times while we were there like she knew we were coming to take her. At one point, she came over to me while I was sitting in a chair and managed to throw the top half of her body on my lap as she started licking my face. Alan and I looked at each other and decided she might just be what Jake needed.

"Could we borrow Bailey for a while to see if she can help our dog, Jake?" I asked. "It will likely be temporary until Jake shows improvement, and then, we'd bring her back."

They both rushed to say, "Yes!"

I think they were only partly relieved, because as much as they wanted Bailey adopted, the couple became teary-eyed as we loaded Bailey into our car.

The behaviorist we had consulted in Saugerties with all those Labradors was right...to a point. Jake took to Bailey, but only when we weren't in the room. Spying through the double doors from the den into the living room, we could see the two of them harmlessly wrestling and playing tug of war with the plush toys. It was so refreshing to see Jake behave like a dog, living in the moment and free of fear.

But as soon as we reappeared, Jake went into his crouched, cowering stance while Bailey happily bolted over to us. *What to do?*

"This situation isn't tenable," Alan said as if he was reading my mind.

"Let's give it a few days and see if there is improvement. Who knows, by the end of the week, Jake may not have a problem with us being in the room as long as Bailey is around." And as soon as I said this, we both realized we had potentially committed ourselves to being a two-dog family, something we hadn't considered and weren't ready for.

A week painfully passed with no improvements. It was like a switch went off in Jake as soon as one of us made an appearance. The fact that Bailey came over to us did not influence Jake at all. He was too afraid.

Finally, after much discussion and tears—mine—we decided to give Jake away. However, it wasn't going to be to just anyone or anyplace because he had such special needs. It would have been easier if he was missing a limb or some other physical abnormality. But this was a defect deep inside him that could be unfixable, and he needed to go somewhere where they understood this.

The summer before we married, Alan and I had taken a trip to Best Friends Animal Sanctuary in Kanab, Utah. It's a beautiful place set in Angel Canyon near the southern border of the state. For those not familiar, Best Friend's provides shelter and rehabilitation to domesticated animals and wildlife. Alan had been a member for several years, so he gave them a call.

Although Best Friends was at capacity, they realized the urgency of our situation and how ill-equipped we were to take care of such a dog. They agreed to take him, and off he went. Although skeptical at first about our assertions that Jake was un-adoptable, our fears were confirmed when we visited Best Friends two years later.

At that time, his caretaker said to us, "Jake will likely live out his life here. He doesn't have the disposition to be placed in a home."

I had breathed a sigh of relief. I was glad we had another chance to see Jake and how happy he was. We took him for a short walk, and he acted no differently from when we'd first gotten him, constantly pulling away from me, walking in a crouched posture. But once he was put back in the dog run with his pals, he stood up straight and playfully engaged with them.

His caretaker shared that after spending two years with Jake, he had finally stopped trying to get away from her when she entered his pen or took him for walks. Needless to say, we were happy about how it turned out for Jake and felt fortunate that he led us to Bailey!

LEARNING: Much of a dog's formative development occurs within the first few months of its life. This is when a dog typically forms its perspective of the world as it directly experiences it. This includes socialization with other dogs, people, places, and things.

Ideally, exposing your dog to as much as possible in these first months can make all the difference and

Last Dog

make life more enjoyable for them and an easier one for you! Constant exposure to new experiences will also help your dog learn how to easily adapt to new experiences throughout its life.

For example, I have a friend with a ten-year-old goldendoodle named Maggie who had rarely slept overnight in any house other than her own. Maggie just recently visited our house for an overnight. My friend wasn't sure why Maggie was so anxious that evening. She didn't touch the fresh marrowbone I'd given her, and the following morning, she shadowed my friend's every move. Nothing she did for her seemed to help. I told her I suspected Maggie was anxious to be away from home and would probably be less so once she got in the car.

I turned out to be right. Once Maggie saw she was heading to the car, her mood improved, and she couldn't wait to get in, jumping into the front passenger seat. She sat looking straight ahead, I suspect with only one thing on her mind—going home!

I have also known dogs that were seldom or if ever taken for a walk. The only time they went out of the house was to be taken to the vet or playgroup by car. When they were finally taken for a walk in their neighborhood, they barked at parked and passing cars, people standing outside their house, the occasional slammed door, etc. This perspective of the world was new to them, and most adult dogs typically fear what they are not familiar with.

If they had been able to reverse time and start walking the dog as a puppy, it would approach new experiences with great curiosity and a positive attitude.

Jake, standing in submissive posture with tail down and hind area rounded.

CHAPTER 2: BAILEY

Here to Stay

For Bailey, the bigger the stick, the better!

What originally started out as our "bull in a china shop" eventually grew up to be a well-behaved, friendly, extremely smart and beautiful Labrador. Bailey wasn't the typical-looking, chocolate Labrador. The sun had painted her coat with golden highlights by late spring. She had a medium, stocky frame, and square-shaped head. At times, she could look intimidating and at other times, totally adorable.

Topping off her unique looks was a splash of white fur sitting on her chest, fully visible like a badge. I used to call it her "sweet spot," because when anyone petted Bailey there, she would slowly close her eyes as though she were in heaven.

Several weeks after picking up Bailey, we called the couple who had fostered her.

"I wanted to let you know that Bailey is doing great, and if you haven't changed your mind, we'd like to adopt her. You can visit Bailey any time," I said.

The couple sounded relieved to hear this. I suspect that during their time away from Bailey, they had realized their original decision to get her adopted was the right one after all. A few weeks passed, and the woman called to ask if she could come by to see Bailey with her granddaughter, who had gotten along very well with Bailey.

"Of course," I said, half-worried that the little girl would start whining for Bailey to come back home with them.

When they showed up, Bailey greeted them like old friends, running over and pushing her body into them as if she were giving a hug. The little girl squealed with delight as Bailey excitedly licked her face from top to bottom and side to side all the while frantically wagging her tail.

"I'm grateful to you for giving Bailey a good home. It's comforting to know Bailey is nearby, the woman told me." But despite our close proximity, she never visited again.

Luckily, Alan and I were home a lot, because we were both freelancing and had the luxury of time to properly train Bailey. Given how smart Bailey was, and that she so eager to please, she wasn't difficult to train.

Within a couple of months, we had her walking off-leash during our hikes in the mountains. Quite overweight when she came to us, we knocked off thirty-plus pounds to get her to a "fighting weight" of sixty-

Last Dog

five pounds. We fed her lean food, scaled back on treats, and denied her human food during those first six months. Coupled with a few all-day hikes per week, she not only lost weight but also built up muscle. She basically turned into what I call a calendar dog.

Bailey enjoyed being the only dog in our home; she actually seemed to luxuriate in it! She proved to be excellent companionship on those wintry days and nights when one of us was at home alone. This was a big transition since Alan and I were both new to the quiet solitude of rural life. And Bailey kept *us* fit. A day never went by that we didn't take her for a walk—snow, rain, or shine.

During the first several years of our marriage, Bailey benefited from Alan and I being unencumbered by the demands of a full-time staff job. We were able to take three weeks off at a time and pack up the van for one of our many cross-country hiking trips. The first was to Newfoundland, followed by several trips to the American Southwest and the South and all the states in between. Bailey traveled very well in cars, on ferries, and in elevators once she got over the sensation of the ground moving beneath her paws.

In addition, Bailey accompanied us on several journeys to Block Island, Rhode Island, which became our home away from home. It was during one of our visits that we hiked to the Great Salt Pond. At the time, the tide was out so we could walk for several yards with the water level never getting higher than mid-thigh. Since adopting Bailey, we had tried several times to coax her into the water without success. Either there was too much action in the water—like water rushing too fast in one of the streams upstate or ocean waves—

or her paws couldn't reach the lakebed. But the pond was perfect for Bailey to get her sea legs. Coaxing her in did not work, because all she did was bark and resist.

"Fine, suit yourself, but we're going for a swim," I said to her as if she could understand.

As we turned our backs on Bailey to walk out farther into the pond, she barked more intensely, as if she were yelling, "Come back."

I have a great picture of Bailey, standing in the high grass just off the pond's shore in a defiant stance, barking her head off. I chuckle every time I look at it.

One of the times I turned back to glance at our barking Bailey, I could not believe what I saw. I called to Alan, who was just ahead of me, to turn around.

Bailey had apparently tossed aside her fear, stubbornness, or pride and had walked out into the water toward us. Once she lost her footing, her canine instincts kicked in, and she swam the doggy paddle. Alan and I were thrilled and stopped to wait for her to catch up to us.

"What a good girl. You see, you can do it!" we excitedly praised as she reached us.

With that, she began showing off by swimming around us several times as if to say, "Hey, look guys, see what I can do!"

LEARNING: Do you know the saying, "You can't teach an old dog new tricks"? Well, scratch that one off the list. It isn't true. It wasn't true for any of our dogs, even for the oldest dog we adopted, who was seven and a half years old. I will get to that in a later chapter.

Evidently, Bailey didn't have the chance to experience water in her puppyhood when it is ideal to

Last Dog

expose them to as much as possible. We were told by our vet and discovered through our readings that the likelihood of getting an adult dog—even a dog bred for the water—was not in our favor. But we did it, and not by throwing her in.

The trick is to get the dog devoted to you, the pack leaders. Through this devotion, they will want to please you and always be with you no matter how difficult the challenge or how stubborn they are as was in Bailey's case. The secret is patience, discipline, and love.

This formula works regardless of what you are trying to achieve with your furry friend—walking off-leash, commands, behavior modification, etc. You need to let your dog know what you want and give them direction, because that is what they need. As in a wolf pack, the alpha and beta are constantly giving direction, rebuke, and rewards. That is how they maintain the respect and loyalty of the pack members.

WATCHING ALAN and Bailey hiking together was like watching a boy and his dog. At first whenever we hiked, Bailey would walk just behind Alan, struggling to catch up. But after a few months, Bailey was in her stride out ahead of both of us, leading the way as she was in such fine shape!

While it's reassuring to have a dog that stays close by your side during a hike, it can become dangerous, as it did one day during our trip to Newfoundland.

Alan is a kid at heart, especially when he is in the great outdoors. He is constantly exploring. And while there are places that are okay for him to explore, it is not necessarily so for dogs. It was a hike that had taken us to one of the many shorelines of Newfoundland. It was a beautiful spot and a perfect one for a rest and some lunch.

Afterward, Alan itched to explore some more but I was still content to take in the scenery. He decided to strike out on his own and climb up a nearby rocky cliff. Of course, as he went, Bailey dutifully followed behind. We assumed she would stop and sit at the base of the cliff when she saw where Alan was going.

But to our surprise, she followed Alan up the cliff. I was concerned. Alan thought if she was willing to go, we should let her, and she'd stop when she couldn't go any farther.

But the holes in that theory immediately became apparent as Bailey managed to climb as high as Alan, ending up right next to him. When Alan realized he couldn't go any farther, he started to descend, but Bailey was stuck.

Obviously, dogs aren't suited for rock climbing, and the descent presented even more challenges. If she turned the wrong way, she could fall. Bailey started to whimper, and my heart was in my throat. I wasn't sure how long she could hold on. Alan started to climb back up to her, speaking reassuringly while trying to get his hand on the scruff of her neck to guide her down. But she wouldn't have it.

"Perhaps we should push her off, and I'll catch her," I suggested.

Alan gave me a look as if he was reconsidering why he had married me.

But what were we to do? I was beside myself. I had an urge to climb right up that rock face, take Bailey in my arms, and bring her down safely.

As seconds passed, Bailey became even more panicked and started to shake. Maybe there was no

Last Dog

choice but to go with my suggestion after all.

At that point, I heard the distant voices of some folks coming off the trail. Maybe they had something in their hiking gear we could retrofit to help get Bailey out of this mess. Upon seeing our predicament, they immediately rushed over. One of the younger guys crawled up the rock face with a rope and tied it around Bailey's body. He led her down toward Alan. She was pretty steady for the first few steps, but then her nerves got the better of her. Bailey's legs gave way, and she fell off.

Luckily, she was close to the ground at that point and landed where I waited for her. Other than being shaken up, the worst she had suffered was a broken nail. The valuable lesson we learned from that moment on is just because a dog wants to do something, it doesn't mean it can or should!

Bailey's greatest pleasure was to fetch sticks, the bigger the better. Sometimes, they were almost as long as her. She was given to retrieving more than one at a time, especially when swimming.

Alan loved to tease Bailey and throw out one stick after another while she frantically swam around to retrieve them all. Just when she'd think she had finished, Alan would throw out yet another stick behind her.

You could sense her frustration as she turned around to retrieve yet another stick! How she managed it without losing one amazes me to this day. I think the game gave Bailey, a working dog, a sense of purpose. You could see how proud she was as she carried her retrieved sticks back to shore as if she felt a sense of accomplishment.

LEARNING: I can't say this enough. Dogs need a sense of purpose. All dogs do. Often, this is achieved through regular walks. For a dog bred for specific jobs, like retrieving/hunting, herding or pulling, the closer the experience matches the work they were bred for, the happier the dog.

I have a friend who had an Australian shepherd named Roux. She took Roux to a herding farm for the day, and she said he was in his glory. The herding instinct had kicked right in! For Bailey, it was retrieving sticks.

But even if we never threw a stick for her to retrieve, she gained a sense of purpose by going on daily walks. Sniffing and tracing a scent is great for any dog, from the smallest to the largest, from the youngest to the oldest.

I believe our dogs, especially those that lived into their teens, retained the disposition of a younger dog because they were mentally stimulated by the daily walks, hikes, and games that we had played with them.

WHEN WE had Bailey, Alan was a partner in a small bar/music venue called The Goldhawk in Hoboken, New Jersey. In those first years, we didn't serve food, so we were able to bring Bailey along during the day while Alan was doing paperwork or in the evenings when we were open for business.

The customers seemed to get a kick out of seeing her, especially the female customers. One customer in particular took a great liking to Bailey and spent a good part of the time with her while she was at the bar.

A few days later, Alan's partner told him there was

Last Dog

a package that had arrived at The Goldhawk addressed to Bailey. We couldn't imagine who could have sent it. When Alan opened it, there was a small card signed by the young girl Bailey had met in the bar a few nights before. The card read how much she enjoyed meeting Bailey, and that she was a beautiful, sweet dog. Inside the box was a stuffed toy and treats.

This wasn't the first time Bailey had won the hearts of people she had just met. During our trip to Newfoundland in a small town named Brigus, we stayed at a B&B run by an older woman. She took an instant liking to Bailey, as did a group of college-age girls checking into the B&B that evening. They asked if they could take her for a walk before going to bed.

"Sure," we quickly responded, as we both welcomed the short reprieve from minding Bailey. They were out for quite a while, over an hour.

"Do you think that was a good idea after all? Those girls are complete strangers. They could have run off with her," I asked as we lay in bed waiting for them to return.

"We're in Brigus, not the Bronx," Alan reassured me.

Soon after, we could hear them come back. I ran down to thank them and took an exhausted Bailey up to bed.

The following morning, Bailey headed downstairs before us; I guess the smells of breakfast cooking were too irresistible for her to resist. I made my way down to see what she was up to. Bailey was sitting in the kitchen in front of the owner of the B&B, who was busy at the stove.

"Someone would like to know if it's okay for them

to have a piece of bacon," she said to me jokingly as she dangled it in front of Bailey.

How could I say anything other than, "Of course she can, thank you."

Bailey snapped it up posthaste!

Bailey taught us a lot about dogs in those first few years. I like to think of her as our first dog; at least, she was the first to live out its life with us.

~*~

We learned even more about Bailey and dogs, when we again became a two-dog household.

After having Bailey for a few years, our lives became busier and we weren't at home with her as much as we would have liked. We had decided to consider getting another dog so Bailey wasn't home alone when we were gone for a stretch of time.

Since Bailey had been fostered in a household with cats and got along well with them and seemed to have gotten along with Jake, we knew we could consider getting another dog as a companion and playmate for her. Even though Bailey considered us her pack, we didn't think it was the same as having another dog around.

Our search began. First, we found a golden retriever mix that was more mix than retriever. He was at a local shelter upstate. He had been found roaming the streets down near New York City and was taken in by one of the local shelters there, but they were at capacity. So he'd been found a new home at this shelter upstate. We named him Luke.

However, we soon discovered that Luke had severe separation anxiety, and it was more than we were willing to manage. Although not his fault, Luke's fits of anxiety terrorized Bailey. I'd often find her sitting in the corner, trembling. When I'd come home, I would find things thrown about, ripped apart, or busted through, like a door. It looked like the results of a demolition team.

Once, I left Luke in the basement while running out to do some errands, thinking it would minimize the potential damage. Well, I was wrong. When I returned, the basement door, which was mostly made of particle board, had been broken through. He had seen me leave through there and was determined to follow me.

Alan and I consulted yet another dog behaviorist who specialized in dogs with separation anxiety. She recommended what I considered an elaborate plan.

"What you need to do is prepare several Kong balls filled with frozen peanut butter to keep him busy while you're gone," she instructed.

I asked her half-jokingly, "Should I to do this even when I go upstairs to take a shower?"

"If that's what it takes," she said to my surprise.

It ended up that Alan and I had to coordinate our comings and goings in and out and around the house to avoid one of Luke's fits. The situation was impossible. This plan wasn't solving anything. I couldn't go the Kong ball route because we'd have another severely overweight dog in no time!

Sadly, we had to return Luke to the shelter. I remember the look of disappointment on the staff's face. I'm sure they thought we hadn't given him enough time.

"Luke's fits are so severe that he's damaging the house and terrorizing my other dog," I explained to the shelter staff.

This poor guy had had a rough start in life, and I wished we had the capacity to help him. I had called the shelter a few days ahead of returning him. They had been able to arrange for a retired military veteran who was experienced in training dogs for military service to foster Luke and hopefully cure him of his anxiety. Needless to say, this made me feel much better about returning him.

 LEARNING: It is sort of like the "chicken and the egg" syndrome. Some dogs are prone to anxiety when left alone, and we enable it by constantly being in their company in an effort to calm them. I have friends with dogs who are so attached to them that when they leave the room, the dog whimpers and searches the house for them. Another friend's dog would bark in the house from the moment she or her husband left for work until they returned that evening. They didn't realize this until their neighbors lost patience and finally told them they'd have to fix the problem or they'd report them.

Knowing what we know now, it's in the best interest of your dog to regularly experience moments of being left behind at home for just short periods of time early on in the relationship. It's not the same as dropping them off somewhere like at daycare, because they are usually distracted and at a place they enjoy. It's quite different to leave them alone in the house. It's best for you and your dog to have this time away from one another and for the dog to know that it's okay to be alone. And don't let those sad, "what will I do without you" looks weaken your resolve. Remain strong!

Last Dog

OUR NEXT find was a chocolate Labrador named Hunter. His family had decided reluctantly that they needed to find him a new home after the birth of their first child. Hunter was an adult dog about four years old, and the couple had him since he was a pup. He had been their "baby" up until now, and this was the problem. Hunter found it difficult to adjust to the new hierarchy, and they were not comfortable having him around their newborn.

The unfortunate thing in all of this was the dog was suffering the sins of their owner. They had allowed Hunter to be the beta to the wife's alpha. The husband had taken a back seat both literally and figuratively.

"He likes to sit in the front seat of the car, so my husband sits in the back while I drive," the wife told us.

Alan and I shot each other a look.

"What happens when you put him in the back seat?" I asked.

"You really can't because he will just push his way into the front seat. If you don't let him up front, he throws a fit while you are driving in the car," she answered very matter-of-factly as if this was acceptable behavior.

"Well, Hunter is going to have to get used to sitting in the back seat with us," Alan announced with certainty.

Little did we know, this king-sized, muscle-bound Labrador that weighed at least a hundred pounds was going to have his way whether we liked it or not.

Despite learning this, we decided to give Hunter a try. We scheduled a second meeting for Bailey and Hunter to get acquainted on neutral territory. We enlisted the help of a dog behaviorist/trainer to supervise and observe any potential issues that might have prevented these two from living in the same household.

Bailey was oblivious to Hunter; she was too busy smelling the scents of the dog run. Hunter *really* liked Bailey, following her very closely. Even though Bailey was spayed, Hunter was *not* neutered. Alan and I put this on the to-do list if we decided to keep Hunter. Male dogs that are not neutered can be much more challenging to discipline, train, and can be aggressive toward other dogs and even people.

After the two met, we went back to the couple's home to pick up Hunter's belongings and take him with us. I could tell they were half-hoping we'd decided not to take him, because they were attached to Hunter.

"Please call if you have any questions. If for some reason it doesn't work out, we don't mind taking him back and finding him another home," the wife said a thousand times.

With that, off we went with Hunter in the back seat. That was problem number one, which we realized immediately as we got on the road. I drove so Alan could play referee in case Hunter got out of hand.

Well, no sooner did we pull out of the driveway than Hunter started pushing through the opening between the front bucket car seats. Luckily, we'd the foresight to put Bailey in the back hatch area to keep her out of harm's way.

The struggle continued the entire, hour-long ride home. Hunter would not let up. I was afraid we were going to get into an accident. What we must have looked like driving up the New York State Thruway, battling this determined dog, lunging forward from the

Last Dog

back seat!

By the time we reached home, Alan and I were exhausted. We put Hunter on a leash and led him around to explore the back yard. Alan took him for a walk because he was way too strong for me, and Alan needed to establish a bond.

The weekend we had Hunter seemed longer than it was but a blur all at the same time. I can only describe how Alan and I felt at the end of it—like dried husks. The final straw came that Monday. I was alone at home with Bailey and Hunter. By this point, Bailey had had enough of Hunter, because he kept trying to mount her, and she would have none of it. She'd bark at him fiercely, but that only made Hunter more adamant about humping her.

Then, he changed his game plan while I was in the living room adjusting the cushions on our love seat. I was slightly bent over when Hunter came from behind and tried to mount me. He knocked me onto the love seat, sending it sliding into the wall. I had never been so startled and frightened by a dog before in my life!

I turned around and yelled at Hunter. I grabbed him with both hands by the scruff of his neck and dragged him into the screened-in porch, shutting the door and locking it behind me!

Bailey sat, looking at me as if she were stunned as well.

I went over and pet her. "Don't worry, sweetie, that spoiled brat is going back where he came from," I reassured her.

Then I called Alan and told him what had happened. I said emphatically, "He is going back. I will not have a dog mount me in my own home or anywhere else for that matter!"

Alan couldn't believe it. I think I heard him chuckle at the other end of the phone. But all in all, he agreed. Alan had enough, too.

The couple was more than happy to come to our house the next day and pick up Hunter. You could tell they missed him and he them. They apologized for any inconvenience he may have caused us. *May? Are they kidding?* That was the understatement of the decade!

"It wasn't really a good fit for Bailey," Alan diplomatically replied. And off they went, with Hunter in the front passenger seat and the husband dutifully sitting in the back seat. Hunter had gotten what he wanted—to go back home and be the king!

LEARNING: In the wolf pack, the importance of hierarchy is an essential tenet that is learned at a young age by each member to promote the health and survival of the pack. Those in the pack that don't behave according to their rank are reprimanded and sometimes severely treated. In extreme instances, a wolf can be run out of the pack and forced to strike out on its own. This could result in the wolf's premature death because it's difficult for a lone wolf to survive very long.

The importance of your dog knowing its place in the pack is essential for a satisfying relationship and day-to-day co-existence. Your dog should never think it's the pack leader. This is a recipe for disaster. At worst, it could put you and your family in a dangerous situation if the dog has an unstable temperament. At the very least, it will create stress, frustration, and unhappiness that could result in your pet being surrendered to a shelter. It could dissuade you from ever adopting a dog again.

Most domesticated dogs are not natural alphas. Their true disposition is more suited for taking direction, but if allowed, they might try to assert themselves and do a bad job of it. In cases like these, dogs may misbehave by lashing out in aggression. They may experience anxiety, and on some level, experience fear.

In Hunter's case, his owners were nervous about having him around the baby. This was not Hunter's fault. His owners were at fault, because they let him try to become the alpha. Your dog should immediately learn that a new pack member, especially a vulnerable newborn, is further up in the hierarchy than it is.

If your child is old enough to be walking, don't hesitate to put a leash in his or her hand and let the child walk the dog around inside the house—supervised of course. This will reinforce your child's higher position in the pack. Have the child give the dog its bowl at feeding time.

Dogs know "which side their bread is buttered on" and have a special reverence for the one who feeds them. Eventually, your child assumes the beta position in the pack, a position your dog will readily respect.

Alan and Bailey taking in the scenery off Clay Head Trail, Block Island.

Bailey the surfer girl.

CHAPTER 3: BAILEY AND RALF

Then There Were Two

Ralf, making himself at home.

We had all but given up the idea of a companion for Bailey. Since we'd struck out twice with Luke and Hunter, we'd reconciled ourselves to sticking with just one dog. Besides, Bailey was enough dog for us first-timers. It didn't appear she was in need of canine companionship.

We'd had Bailey for about three years, and she would turn five years old that June. But that was a ways off as it was now January and the weather had been brutal. We'd had snow on the ground since November and the temperatures consistently hovered between the single digits and teens.

But that didn't stop us. We walked Bailey every day. She was built for this weather with a thick down-like undercoat that kept her extra warm, making her seem impervious to the cold. If we threw snow on her, she would kick into high gear and start running around, celebrating the brisk sensation. When she became warm during a winter hike, she'd simply roll around in the snow until she was sufficiently cooled. And when available, she would treat herself to a quick dip into what was assuredly a freezing cold lake.

Toward the end of that January, I was working in New York City, and Alan was at our house upstate with Bailey. Later that evening, we met in the city for dinner for my birthday. Alan mentioned that he had seen a large, black dog in the orchards adjacent to our backyard that afternoon. Our "backyard" was made up of about five hundred acres of orchard behind our house that serve as a perfect place to walk our dogs off-leash.

Alan said, "I spotted him near the opening just when you come out of the woods into the orchard. Bailey was ready to run over, but the other dog got up and growled. He was much bigger than Bailey, so I decided to take her home and go back and check out this guy on my own.

"When I returned, he let me get a bit closer but still growled. When he stood up this time, it was obvious he'd been on his own for awhile because I could see the outline of his ribs."

When we returned home the next morning, Alan was anxious to take me back to the spot where he had encountered this dog. I doubted he'd still be there and was reluctant to make the trek in snow that was well above my knees, but Alan convinced me that it was the right thing to do.

To my surprise, when we arrived at the spot where

Last Dog

Alan had seen him the day before, he was still there. I saw his big, black head rise up from the snow mound that partially hid where he was camping out. He did not growl this time; I'm not sure why.

"This dog may be less threatened by females. You should try to approach him on your own, but go slowly," Alan cautioned.

I couldn't resist the offer. He had such a sweet face. As I approached, he got up and started to wag his tail. I could see how painfully thin he was for such a big guy.

To my shock, I saw he was making a home and staying warm in the hide of a deer carcass. He was a mess and stunk to high heaven, but I fell in love with him on the spot. He tried to walk over to me, but his back left leg wobbled. I quickened my pace to him, and when we met, he pushed first his head and then his body into me. I immediately petted him, but the stench coming from him was unbearable.

"We need to get him out of here, but how? The orchard road isn't plowed and our car can't get through here," I yelled back to Alan.

"Let's get in touch with the neighbors up the road and see if we can borrow their pickup truck," Alan recommended.

I felt awful leaving him there, but we had no choice. We quickly headed back home and drove up the road to our neighbor. Although it turned out they were taking their annual holiday abroad, their teenage son and daughter were at the house. As luck would have it, one of their friends, hanging out with them, had a kick-ass, 4x4 truck. We all piled in to rescue this poor guy. As the truck plowed through the snowy, orchard road and made its way closer to him, the dog stood up, started to growl, and bared his teeth. *Not a good sign.* I was worried he would flee and then we'd never find him.

"Stop the truck and let me go over to him alone since he seems to like me. I can lure him into the kennel," I told them.

I had instinctively shoved treats in my pocket before leaving the house earlier and we'd brought along a crate. Going over alone did the trick. He allowed me to pet him while I fed him some treats, and he followed me slowly toward the kennel. He eventually went in as I threw some treats in there. The boys lifted the kennel into the back of the truck, and I hopped in next to the crate and continued to feed him treats.

Upon getting back to the house, we realized we hadn't thought this through.

"We can't take him into the house; he's so dirty and smelly. Besides we're not sure how he and Bailey will get along, if at all," I said to Alan.

Instead, we set up bedding and a space heater in the garage. I ran upstairs to put on old clothes that could be thrown out afterward so I could spend some quality time with this guy. We got him food and water, and once he fell asleep, I went back upstairs.

The following morning, I called the vet's office. I explained our situation, and. they kindly scheduled an appointment for that afternoon. We left him there overnight so our vet, Karen, could give him a full exam.

Alan and I returned to the vet's office the following afternoon. They were still waiting for blood test results, and his urine showed he had a UTI. Thankfully, he tested negative for parasites in his stool. However, his

Last Dog

left hip was dislocated. That's why it looked wobbly when he walked.

Karen suggested, "Once he's adopted, he should have surgery to remove the top portion of his hip (ball socket) so the muscles and tendons around it can grow and strengthen to keep the leg aligned with the hip. This is better than reinserting the ball into the socket, because it would inevitably pop out again, causing him constant discomfort."

"Let's do it then," I said without hesitation.

"Are you adopting him?" Karen asked.

"I'm not sure, but we can't leave him like this. No one will want to adopt him with this injury," I said without consulting Alan or even myself for a millisecond. I just couldn't fathom doing anything else.

As timing would have it, Alan, Bailey, and I were leaving for a two-week road trip to St. George Island off the coast of the Florida Panhandle. We had no choice but to leave our new friend at the vet. We scheduled Bailey's sitter, Cindy, to visit the vet daily to take him for walks. Karen had reinforced the need for regular exercise after surgery to start building up strength in his leg.

"You're sure you want to do all this while you haven't decided whether or not you are going to keep him?" Karen asked.

"That's right," I replied rather matter-of-factly.

During our drive to St. George Island, I made several check-in calls with the vet's office. The staff gave me enthusiastic updates.

"Everyone at the office just loves having him around. He is so well-behaved that we let him out of his kennel during the day so he can walk around and exercise his leg. By the way, he cleaned up nicely after a couple of baths, and he is a beautiful dog!" the vet tech, Lynn, added.

To be fair, I hadn't given him much thought once we arrived at St. George Island, but when we returned we went to the vet's office straight away. He came out to greet us like old friends.

At that moment, I couldn't imagine giving him away, especially to put him in a shelter situation. His long, feathery tail wouldn't stop wagging, and his whole body seemed to gyrate with joy. He didn't forget us! The staff just couldn't stop talking about how much they loved having him there. I looked at Alan, and he gave me a nod as he knew what I was thinking.

"So have you decided on whether or not you are going to keep him?" the vet asked.

"Yes," I blurted. "We're taking him home."

And with that we were off.

"I hope Bailey will be okay with this," Alan half-joked.

Bailey was okay with it—eventually. Bailey had enjoyed being the only dog in our family and having another dog in the house challenged her position in the pack. She wouldn't readily engage with him, behaving as if he was beneath her. He tried time and again to get her to play. He would often nudge Bailey to the point of getting her so exasperated that she'd chase after him out of anger, nipping at him. He took no mind, as he playfully ran back and forth perhaps thinking, this was better than nothing.

Without consulting Alan, I quickly named our black, smooth, long-coated friend Ralf. But I called him Ralfie. It seemed to fit his goofy disposition perfectly.

Last Dog

Everything about Ralf seemed out of place. No one was exactly sure of his breed or the mix that gave him his unique look.

He stood tall with his head up just past my hip, and I stand at about five feet and three inches. He was long, almost twice the length of Bailey. He had a huge, block-shaped head and small eyes. His ears were smallish for his head and were fringed, as was his tail and the backside of his legs, similar to an Irish Setter. And when the sun hit his coat just right, you could see red highlights on his fur fringe. He had huge, clumsy paws. Karen thought he was a flat-coated retriever but larger than most. I think he was a mutt with some Rottweiler, which would explain his block head, and Irish setter, which would explain his fringed, wavy coat and long, lanky body. And perhaps there was a little Newfoundland thrown in. All we knew was he was a goofy, adorable, and loveable guy! We were so glad he landed on our doorstep so to speak, because the next fifteen months were jam-packed with adventure.

Ralf quickly made himself at home. He seemed downright comfortable from the start. After Ralf's hip surgery, we started him on the road to recovery with daily walks, slowly building up his strength so he could eventually begin hiking with us in the mountains.

It took only a few months before we made our first trip to the Shawangunks, and by late March, it was warm enough for these guys to go swimming. Bailey, as you know, had successfully gotten over her fear of water. Mind you, we'd thought she was an anomaly. I mean, a Labrador that's afraid of the water…c'mon!

But we seemed to have a knack for beating the odds on this issue, because Ralf was also not so fond of the water. He had no desire to follow Bailey into Lake Minnewaska. This was surprising, because he followed Bailey everywhere, so desperate was he to get her to accept him. But the good part was that Ralf had made the two-mile hike all the way around the lake without a problem.

During our walks, Ralf now garnered attention because of his unusual looks and goofy disposition. At first, some folks were tentative to approach because of his size, but once they saw his long fringed tail wagging frantically and his block-shaped head bouncing side-to-side as he trotted over to say "hello," their fear quickly melted away.

I may be projecting, but I don't think Bailey was too happy about this. She was used to getting all the accolades. This shift in attention was also starting to happen in our home as Ralf became more my dog. But Bailey still had Alan as her buddy to throw her blue, rubber ball far out into the backyard, tease her with a game of fetch sticks in the water, lead her on a chase after the squirrels to get them away from the bird feeder, and to wrestle or play tug-of-war with at the end of the day.

When Bailey did feel playful toward Ralf, she would get into an intense tug-of-war play session coined the "tractor pull." Basically, Ralf would lay on his side, holding the plush toy—a.k.a. "woobie"—between his teeth for dear life at one end, and Bailey would stand while pulling from the other. She would pull Ralf clear across the floor from the living room into the den, all eighty-five pounds of him! She had jaws of steel with a determination to match.

That summer was Ralf's first road trip with us. We

Last Dog

took a short excursion to our home away from home on Block Island, Rhode Island. It was the first time he'd be in the car for any real length of time, and we were hoping he'd travel as well as Bailey. Hopefully, the sensation of being on a ferry for the one-hour ride would sit well with him. And it did.

Once we made landfall on the other side, we had no doubt he'd love this small gem of an island just as much as the three of us. It seemed as though Ralf's breeding really kicked in once we hit the island. Block Island is abundant with birds and fowl, so Ralf was constantly on the hunt, thankfully never catching anything. His instincts would quickly take over as he'd slowly stalk his intended prey in a low, crouched position through the high grass.

But we had no luck coaxing Ralf to take a swim. We tried the same spot that worked with Bailey. All of us swam in the Great Salt Pond, hoping that Ralf would finally get the hint, but he was too distracted by the bird life, trying to catch a seagull.

By this time, Ralf was in prime shape. The rudder-like wobble in his rehabilitated leg was almost unnoticeable, which meant the muscles around his upper leg and hip were strengthening. We were able to get Ralf up to a healthy weight of eighty-five pounds, which was perfect for his body frame. This was the first dog we had to work at getting weight on instead of off. Luckily, his weight distribution fell more toward the front of his body with his body narrowing near the hips, which helped to avoid putting stress on his compromised leg. Ralf developed into a fine-looking dog, and he was having the time of his life!

The relationship between Bailey and Ralf had

improved by this time. I would describe it as Bailey had learned to tolerate Ralf, as if realizing he was here to stay. She would put up a good front, playing hard-to-get and not wanting to engage at first, Ralf would do something goofy like turn a summersault and her defenses would ultimately give way to play. When Bailey grew tired of Ralf's antics and became impatient, he'd quickly diffuse her anger by licking her ears, sending her into a blissful mood.

Our outdoor adventures continued that summer. Alan was not around as much. He was back to freelancing at his former company. So it was the summer of me, Bailey, and Ralf. Although I had to go into the office a couple of days a week, the majority of my time was happily spent as a dog nanny. Actually, it gave me a nice break from the tempo of a Madison Avenue advertising agency.

One day in early August, we went to the town of High Falls to go swimming since it was the hottest it had been that summer. It's a scenic spot to cool off and a large enough area where we could take the dogs off-leash and be at little risk of bothering anyone.

After all our trips that spring and summer, Ralf had still not ventured into the water. Once I got us settled, I joined Bailey, who was already in the water, swimming. Ralf stood at the water's edge, watching us as usual. I waved to Ralf, and to my surprise, that is all it took. As if he'd done it a hundred times, he casually walked into the water and swam over to me. I could not believe it. I wanted to shout, I wanted to call Alan, and I wanted to celebrate!

"Good boy, Ralfie." I gave him a big kiss on top of that block head of his.

Last Dog

From then on, there was no getting Ralf out of the water for better or for worse.

The following March, Ralf was ready for his first long road trip. We packed up the van and headed out again to the great American Southwest with the two dogs in tow. We made many stops along the way before arriving at our first intended destination in New Mexico.

Winter was still holding onto this heavily forested area in the mid-section of the state. The sweetly pine-scented air hit my nostrils the moment I cracked open the car door. Ralf's quirky habits that came out on this trip made him all the more loveable.

During an overnight stay at one of the many motels we had booked along the way to New Mexico, Alan and I returned to the room after dinner.

"Hey, look at this," Alan pointed to a trail of trash littering the floor upon entering our room. His pointed finger continued to lift all the way back to the bathroom door at the other end of the room.

"What the—?" I asked in amazement. My first thought was someone had come into the room and knocked over the waste basket. But who would break in, rob the place, and take the time to lay out items from the bathroom trash and carefully place them in a line leading to the door of our room?

"One of the dogs must have knocked over the trash," Alan offered.

"Yeah," I agreed, "but that doesn't explain this neatly configured trail. What is this supposed to mean?"

Bailey was passed out on one of the beds, and Ralf was dutifully sitting at my side with his tail brushing back and forth across the floor like a carpet sweeper.

He seemed pleased with himself, waiting for me to praise him for whatever *this* was.

"Well, it must have been Ralf who did this, because we've left Bailey alone several times before in a motel room, and she's never done anything like this," Alan concluded.

I looked down at this sweet guy. "What is this supposed to mean, boy? Is this a gift or something?"

Ralf got up from his sitting position, probably because he thought I was praising him. His tail and lower half of his body wagged and wagged! We couldn't bring ourselves to discipline Ralf, and it wouldn't have made an impact. It was too late after the fact, so he wouldn't have known why he was being reprimanded. Besides, the act was so remarkable, he had half-impressed Alan and me.

However, as we settled into bed later, it occurred to me that Ralf may have been sending a different message altogether.

"I don't think Ralf was happy about us leaving him alone in a strange place. But I don't understand why he didn't push over the can and rip up the refuse in a fit of anger? That would make more sense than this precisely placed trail of trash leading to the motel room door," I said with a yawn.

Alan just gave me a sleepy, "Uh huh," and I put out the light.

This was to be just one of many surprises Ralf had for us during this multi-state hiking trip.

LEARNING: We tend to anthropomorphize when it comes to our pets, giving them human traits. It's easy to draw similarities

Last Dog

to when a child has done something wrong. Whether we witness the mistake happen or learn about it after the fact, we still scold or punish the child. Regardless of the timing, the child usually understands the connection between the scolding and the act.

Dogs can't make the connection unless you are disciplining them when the misdeed is occurring. Instead, they will become confused and connect the scolding to their current behavior. I recommend you don't waste your breath disciplining the dog if you come in after the misbehavior. Although it will be a natural reaction for you to vent at the time of discovering the bad deed, the intention of your disciplining efforts will most likely be lost on your furry friend.

OUR FIRST hiking destination was the small town named Gallup, located in western New Mexico, where we checked into a local motel for a couple of days while exploring the area. This section of New Mexico is part canyon and pine forest with gushing streams. I could feel spring approaching as it was early March. This was indeed a treat, since back home in upstate New York it still looked like tundra country.

We set out the next day for our first hike. We couldn't get used to the fact that we pretty much had the place to ourselves. It was not yet the height of spring vacation season. It was just the four of us and what nature had to offer.

We could hear water gushing loudly as we started along the trail. The distant stream sounded a lot closer because the surrounding canyon magnified the roar of the snow-pack runoff. We could hardly hear each other when we spoke. Bailey sat to the left of me by the stream, watching it go by. When I looked over to my right for Ralf, he wasn't there. Not anywhere for that matter.

"Do you see Ralf?" I shouted to Alan

"No, I thought he was with you," he yelled back.

I instantly panicked. I started yelling his name but my voice was absorbed by the thunderous roar. I walked upstream and then downstream, but found nothing. I decided to continue downstream as there was more of a clearing in that direction. All of a sudden, I saw Ralf's head, bobbing up and down in the water, looking right at me with fear in his eyes while speeding down stream.

"There he is. We're going to lose him down the canyon," I yelled to Alan, pointing.

I went running at top speed, ducking branches and tree limbs while keeping my gaze on that bobbing head. I could see the look of panic on Ralf's face as his flailing front paws tried to get on top of the water, but the stream continued to take him.

A right turn in the bend was coming up. If Ralf passed that point, it would send him down the canyon. The stream's edge I was running on would end in canyon rock face soon. I'd have to jump in to follow him any farther. Out of desperation, I screamed at the top of my lungs, commanding Ralf to get out of the water.

I'm sure he heard the urgency in my voice, because somehow, he managed to muster the strength to direct himself toward the little shoreline to the left side of the bend in the stream. I think the direction of the stream current also helped to push him ashore. I fought my

Last Dog

way through thickets, and as I came through them, Ralf lifted himself up from the water and drunkenly staggered toward me.

The poor guy was beyond saturated. The water in his coat would have doubled his weight. I kneeled down to hug him, and he collapsed in my lap from exhaustion. I covered him with kisses, smothered him with hugs, and nearly saturated myself.

Alan and Bailey showed up behind me, and even Bailey was wagging her tail. Alan was relieved, and he gave Ralf a big hug.

"You big, dummy!" Alan said endearingly. The nickname stuck after that episode.

"This is a good time to find a spot to relax and have some lunch while Ralf takes a well-deserved nap and dries in the warm sun," I suggested.

THE NEXT DAY, we took a hike well away from any water. Instead, we went to a mostly wooded area with some rock face, with the makings for a quiet, leisurely hike. We didn't see a soul until a young couple seemed to appear from out of nowhere, walking their two mules.

The only way to describe them was they looked like mountain people. They had weatherworn, ruddy complexions and hair that looked like it hadn't been combed in years. They seemed just as startled to see us. We waved hello, although neither of them responded.

Ralf had a different idea altogether as he started charging the mules. Alan called after him, commanding him to come back, but it was too late. The mules started to kick with their hind legs, trying to fend Ralf off.

I screamed after him, envisioning one of those

kicks landing on his head and knocking him out cold, or worse. The couple tried to pull their mules away, but Ralf just kept at them. It was tricky for Alan to pull Ralf away without risking a kick or two to the head. Alan grabbed a stick, almost beating Ralf back from the mules. It seemed to do the trick.

We apologized profusely to the couple and conveyed that Ralf meant no harm. They gave us what we interpreted as an understanding nod, a wave of the hand in goodbye, and continued on their way.

"Great, Ralf, you are two for two so far," Alan chided.

"We better keep him on leash for the rest of the trip," I suggested. That idea turned out to be short-lived.

For his final act on this trip, Ralf managed to get skunked. He charged full-speed at one with Bailey not too far behind. At least Bailey had had sense enough to keep a safe distance. She was curious but not stupid.

Wish I could say the same about Ralf. He got what he deserved as far as the skunk was concerned—a full assault to the face and eyes, causing him to yelp and run around blindly.

We spent the rest of our day searching for a general store that sold tomato juice, buying all this "in the middle of nowhere" store had—a total of six large, ancient-looking cans. We stood on the side of this dusty road outside the general store with jugs of water and tomato juice, giving Ralf a bath. It never really got the stink completely out of him—especially the top of his head, which was ground zero—until we could give him a proper bath at home. The rest of the trip was uneventful, thank God.

Just a few days after arriving home from our trip,

Last Dog

we placed Ralf in a dog daycare service along with Bailey. This indoor facility had recently opened near our apartment in Hoboken, New Jersey. It was owned and run by a husband and wife who were friends of a friend. Alan had met the husband while visiting the indoor facility just before we had left for our road trip vacation. Alan had a good feeling about the place and the owner's philosophy about what dogs need.

After having been away for three weeks, we faced a mountain of work and had decided to give the daycare a try. Alan informed them that we didn't know Ralf's background and had only had him for a little more than a year. He specifically instructed that if they experienced any trouble with Ralf to give him a call since his office was in town.

Within a half-hour of leaving, Alan got a phone call from the dog daycare that Ralf had suffered an accident and had died. I couldn't believe it when Alan called me at work. I didn't understand what he was saying.

His words were, "Ralf is gone."

But to me, it wasn't computing. Then he explained the chain of events that caused Ralf's death.

"It was totally avoidable," Alan started. "They told me that Ralf had a bad reaction after I'd left. He was trying to jump the wall in the play area, so one of the attendants decided to put him in a medium, kennel-like enclosure. The gate to the enclosure did not reach the ceiling, so Ralf was able to scale the fencing and get out.

"Instead of the staff calling me like I told them to, they decided to put Ralf in a taller enclosure. This time as he tried to scale the gate, Ralf's collar caught the top part of the gate. He lost his footing and essentially hung himself. This poor guy must have thought I was leaving him behind in a shelter." I could hear Alan choking up at this point, barely getting the words out.

When Alan and I arrived at the facility about an hour later to pick up Ralf's body, I read the staff the riot act.

"You treated our dog like he was a piece of furniture that you needed to get out of the way. Instead of trying to work with him, you shoved him in a kennel," I scolded.

I threatened to sue and go to the local paper with my story. The owner pleaded with us to reconsider, having only been open a few short weeks. The situation was also tricky as they were friends of a close friend of Alan's. They offered us financial compensation for our loss—as if there was an equivalent dollar amount to make up for Ralf's death. Alan accepted, but we informed them that we weren't going to use it for anything other than as a donation to an animal charity supporting dog adoptions.

I had a moment to sit with Ralf's body, petting him for the last time and telling him how much he was loved and how terribly sorry I was that this had happened. We wrapped his body in sheets and loaded him into the back of our wagon.

We drove in silence to our home upstate in a pelting rainstorm that set the appropriate mood for our loss. By the time we arrived home, it was dark, so we pulled the car into the backyard up to the fenced-in area where we were to bury him.

Looking back, it was as if Ralf was not destined to live in this world too long. We had rescued him on death's door, and he had come close to death twice while on vacation. At least he'd had the best fifteen months a dog could ever have.

LEARNING: Dogs are very good communicators. They "wear their hearts on their sleeve" as the saying goes. It is our failure in acknowledging their communication that inevitably leads to problems.

In this instance, the staff at the dog daycare was either inexperienced or lazy or a little of both. Their reaction to Ralf's attempt to communicate his displeasure was met with dismissal at first and then carelessness as they repeated the same action after he'd managed to escape the first kennel. Ralf had been in a panic, and they hadn't invested any effort to try to mitigate the situation by employing behavioral training techniques to calm him. At the very least, they could have called Alan.

A simple precaution like removing his collar when they put him in the kennel would have likely prevented his death. Since then, this dog daycare has made it a policy to remove the collars from those dogs put in a kennel. At our suggestion, they created fabric sleeves fitted across the top of the gate to protect against injury from the fence protrusions.

After hearing our story, the owners of the dog playgroup near our home upstate enacted a policy of no collars in the dog run or the van during transport.

THE SUDDENNESS of Ralf's passing was one of the most difficult losses I had suffered up to that point in my life. As woman on the cusp of forty, many would say that I was lucky if this was the worst loss I'd ever experienced. But I did not feel lucky. All I felt for months was a hole, deep inside me.

You see, Ralf was my dog, and Bailey was Alan's. Ralf always wanted to be with me. If I was in the room with Alan, Ralf would go to me. When Ralf was scared, he'd run behind me. If I was petting Bailey, he would take his mouth and gently remove my hand off her and onto him.

And the same was true of Bailey and Alan—they hiked side by side and wherever Alan went, Bailey followed. She just lit up when he came into the room. And although Bailey sat by me when she sensed I was sad after Ralf had passed away, licking away the tears that often rolled down my face without warning, she was still Alan's dog.

Ralf at Peter's Kill, Minnewaska State Park.

Ralf at Great Salt Pond, Block Island.

Ralf and Bailey, playing tug-o-war.

CHAPTER 4: CHARLIE AND BAILEY

Total Opposites

Charlie and Bailey, interested in sharing our lunch.

With Ralf gone, we truly thought we'd go back to being a one-dog household. The addition of Ralf was great, but he hadn't been planned. So we should just stick to our original plan, right? Well, no. Once you have more than one dog and one of them moves on, there's an empty space that feels uncomfortable, almost begging to be filled. At least, that has been our experience.

Although Bailey was again enjoying being the only dog—or as I called it, "the top dog" in our house—Alan and I needed to fill that big empty space that our Ralf

Last Dog

had left. As I continued to mourn Ralf, Alan went online in search of a male, adult Labrador from a local shelter.

"I found a great looking guy. He's a three-and-a-half-year-old yellow Labrador named Spikey, and he's only been at the shelter for a few weeks. He is well-trained, and his family was forced to give him up because of a move to Florida. I am thinking of going over there tomorrow to check him out," Alan said excitedly over the phone when he called me at work.

After Alan went to see Spikey the following afternoon, he urged me to go with him for a visit that upcoming Saturday, taking Bailey along. I could tell he really wanted this to work out. We arrived early that afternoon. We first went inside without Bailey to check out Spikey on our own. They brought him out in a travel kennel where they left him for a few moments while we waited for the adoption counselor. Spikey barked non-stop until someone who worked there walked over, kicked his kennel, and told him to shut up.

Shooting Alan a look, I asked, "Are you sure he's friendly? That's some bark."

"Yeah, it's probably because he just doesn't like being in that cramped kennel. He was fine when I visited the other day," Alan protested.

One of the counselors finally came over to us. He suggested that we go outside and introduce Spikey to Bailey. So that's what we did. Spikey was in the enclosure and Bailey was outside of it. Spikey barked his head off at Bailey. *Not a good sign.*

"I don't think this match is going to work," the counselor said.

"Well, let's not throw in the towel so fast. Can we

have Bailey go inside the enclosure and see if that makes a difference?" Alan lobbied.

However, the counselor resisted. Alan asked to speak with the manager, and soon after, the manager appeared. After conferring with Alan, she agreed that putting Bailey inside the enclosure with Spikey was worth a try. That's what did the trick! As soon as Bailey was inside, Spikey changed his tune and eagerly followed her around. He seemed smitten. In a blink of an eye, we signed some papers, got Spikey's dossier, and off we went. Bailey rode with me in my car, and Spikey went with Alan in his, all on our way home to embark on another two-dog household adventure.

After arriving home, we allowed Bailey and Spikey to get reacquainted in the backyard. They did just fine, which meant Bailey acted aloof while Spikey followed her closely. With that, we decided it was time to introduce Spikey to his new home. We let him in through the back door and unhooked his leash, allowing him to explore. At some point, we lost track of Spikey.

"Where did he go?" I yelled as I searched upstairs.

"I don't see him down here," Alan yelled up.

I was about to head back downstairs when I saw the cutest thing—Spikey's black nose poking out through the shower curtain of Alan's bathtub. He was inside the bathtub. I walked in and pulled back the shower curtain, looking at him adoringly.

"Are you dropping us a hint? Do you want a bath?" I asked jokingly while reaching to guide him out of the tub.

Once we got downstairs, I said to Alan, "You know, I don't like his name, and it doesn't suit him."

"I know," Alan agreed.

Last Dog

I continued, "Let's give him a name that ends with a similar sound, and he should take to it soon." We sat there and listed different names until one sounded like it fit him. That is how we landed on Charlie. It suited him perfectly!

Charlie had a quiet way about him. I could only describe it as observant, contemplative, as if he was deliberating a decision of some sort. His overall demeanor was subdued. Obviously, he was much different from Ralf, and at first, it was a problem for me.

Charlie wasn't the typical, affectionate Labrador. He was reserved and even-keeled. Back then, I described him as a dog with flattened affect, a description you'd give a person suffering from depression. And maybe at first he was. His previous owners had had him since he was a pup. His first family was the only world he'd known. When they had left him, I am sure the poor guy had been shell-shocked. But we managed to take his mind off this with daily walks, training, and lots of attention.

We got Charlie in May, so it was perfect hiking and swimming weather. We were eager to know if we'd broken our streak of adopting swimming-averse dogs with Charlie. Some weeks later, we took Charlie on his first, full-day hike in the Shawangunks. We'd gotten him into shape by taking him on longer and longer walks over time, which had started to build his stamina and muscle.

We decided he was finally ready for a hike to Awosting Lake, which meant a three-plus-mile hike out there. The backwoods portion of the trail added maybe another half-mile to this. There was also some rock climbing involved. Bailey had done this hike several times and was at her fittest.

Charlie started out great, and we could see how much he was enjoying the trail. He was a sniffer—a painstakingly methodical one. It seemed like every rock, blade of grass and branch was worthy of investigation. As we came to the end of the backwoods trail and rejoined the main trail, I put Charlie back on-leash.

After a few feet, he stopped and sat down. Just like that, he wasn't budging. I could see he was pooped. Alan was ahead of me by several yards, and the lake was less than a quarter of a mile away. Bailey started to trot faster ahead as she could smell the lake water.

Alan shouted back, "C'mon, Cyn, get him up. We're almost there!"

"He won't budge, and I'm nervous about pushing him if he isn't ready. We'll catch up to you. Go ahead," I yelled back.

Charlie sat under the shady tree for a few minutes until he was ready to forge ahead again. I am sure he could smell the lake water, too, and I think that helped shorten his respite in the shade. Then we walked slowly to the lake. To my surprise, Charlie walked right into Awosting Lake, swimming without any coaxing or fanfare. Thank you, Charlie!

Over the years, Charlie made several of these trips to Awosting Lake with Bailey. They became good companions. Charlie didn't push to play all that much, just when it came to their woobies. Charlie would shove a woobie in Bailey's face, and this would get her going. She'd latch on tightly to the opposite end.

At first, both were determined to outlast the other,

Last Dog

but eventually, Charlie would give up. I think Charlie knew it was better for him to lose if it meant he'd get Bailey to play with him more. And Bailey was very happy with this arrangement. They were compatible on hikes, exploring together, and each showing interest in what the other was sniffing. They balanced each other well.

Our next big outing was later that summer to a place called North-South Lake in the Catskill Mountains about forty-five minutes north of our house. We had been up there before with Bailey, and were sure Charlie would like it, too. As the name suggests, there are two lakes and a long trail that wraps around both. There would be more than enough to keep us and the dogs busy during our day visit. We decided to let Bailey and Charlie go for a swim before we set out on a hike.

As soon as we let Charlie off-leash, he took off and leapt into the lake. Charlie paddled quite fast to reach the center of the lake to a family of five ducklings, minding their own business. They eventually saw Charlie coming at them head-on and started to speed away.

"He'll never reach them," Alan said with a half laugh. "Charlie will run out of gas before they do."

That thought scared me. Could a dog—a Labrador nonetheless—drown in a lake?

With that, I started to call out, "Charlie, come back here. Treats, I have treats." But to no avail. I turned to Alan. "What are we going to do?"

"Oh, don't worry. He'll figure it out," Alan reassured.

And he was right. Thankfully, it finally registered

with Charlie that he was not going to get his muzzle on any of those ducks. They quacked as they paddled away from Charlie. One of the parents—likely the father since he was the more colorful of the two adults—turned around and headed at Charlie while the rest of the family continued on their way. I think this duck's unexpected maneuver, coupled with Charlie's tiring legs, made him decide to turn around toward the shoreline back to us. Needless to say, once Charlie rejoined us, he needed a good rest before resuming our hike.

Charlie had grown into a fine dog. His frame filled out with muscle tone, and he was at his peak of fitness, able to conquer several-mile hikes without a problem. His coat was smooth as silk and a brilliant, yellowy-white accented with warmer hues of taupe and brown. His eyes were coal black and contrasted nicely with his yellow face. He had jowls that cloaked his neck beautifully, especially when he lay on his stomach and his head was up looking straight at us. Charlie looked regal.

Charlie was an excellent watchdog, sounding a bark the moment he heard an unusual sound. He would bark until he had our attention, and he'd accompany us while we'd inspect the cause of the noise. He certainly made me feel safer when I was home on my own.

Charlie immediately started joining Bailey on her twice-weekly playgroup dates. We were told by the owners of the playgroup that many of the dogs would try to mount Charlie since he was new and not yet confident. But over time, Charlie—with Bailey's help since she was the dominant one at home as well as at the play group—grew more confident, and the mountings by the other dogs eventually stopped. In later years when Bailey was no longer with us, Charlie would reportedly mount the others dogs in the playgroup. Perhaps he was taking over for Bailey as she had been deemed "Queen Humpadora" of the playgroup by Emily, one of the owners.

LEARNING: If not in a mating situation, dogs will typically mount each other to establish dominance. Even dogs of the same sex will mount each other for this very reason. The dog who is doing the mounting is communicating that it's top dog in the pack hierarchy. This mounting may occur frequently when a new dog enters a pack.

This was the case for Charlie when he initially joined the playgroup. If the mounted dog does not put up much of a resistance or is conveying a submissive energy or posture, that dog can be a target for serial mountings by not only the top dog but also by other members in the group.

This pecking order is not necessarily permanent. It's dependent on the submissive dog to assert itself and convey a different energy to change the dynamic and stop the mounting.

IN TERMS of training, Charlie was the type of dog you only had to reprimand once and he'd never do the bad deed again. For example, when we first got him, I had chicken breasts defrosting on the kitchen counter. Luckily, my trip back into the kitchen coincided with Charlie leaping up against the edge of the counter, trying to get the defrosting chicken breasts.

Cynthia Flowers

"Charlie, get down!" I shouted.

I must have startled him, because he lost his balance and tumbled backward with the plate of chicken following him to the floor. That was the first and last time Charlie ever tried anything like that!

Early on, Charlie had the occasional habit of disappearing from the backyard. We'd be reading or doing some yard work in the backyard and suddenly notice he wasn't around. We'd check the front yard but would find no sign of him. We'd yell out his name and walk to the back section of the yard. It was too difficult to see beyond the fields of wild flowers that stood almost four feet or higher by mid-summer. And then after some time, he would suddenly reappear.

It continued to be a mystery to us until one day later that summer. I was walking Charlie and Bailey on-leash down a side road just beyond our house. It's a relatively quiet, country road that we would sometimes take to access the back orchards when the path through the woods became too buggy and overgrown.

The neighbor living in the house next to the orchard entrance happened to be outside with her two dogs that day. I soon learned that one of them was a female named Ruby. The dog made a move to walk over, but her owner grabbed her by the collar to prevent her from going into the road. At the same time, Charlie pulled toward the dog.

"I know that guy," she said as she pointed to Charlie.

"Oh, I don't know about that. We just adopted him a little over a month ago from a shelter in New Jersey," I replied diplomatically.

As Charlie got closer, she exclaimed, "I do know

that guy, because he comes to visit Ruby. He comes out from over there." She indicated the orchard entrance. "I would try to grab him by the collar to see his ID tags, but he would pull away from me."

The mystery had been solved. This is where Charlie disappeared to when he went missing in our backyard.

A few weeks later, my sister, Claudia, was visiting for the weekend. She was relaxing on a lounge chair in the backyard, reading, and I had stepped inside to get a refill of iced tea for the two of us. When I came back out, Charlie was nowhere to be found. I asked Claudia about it, but she hadn't noticed that he'd slipped away. Charlie was very stealth-like.

I called out, "Charlie. Charlie, treats!" But I heard nothing.

And then, I remembered what my neighbor had said.

I told Claudia, "I think I know where he went. I'll be right back."

I jumped in the car, drove down that road I had been walking Charlie and Bailey down not too long ago, and pulled into the orchard entrance with the hopes of cutting Charlie off at the pass. I got out of the car and waited for "Casanova" to emerge from the woods.

Only a minute or two had passed before Charlie emerged happily, intending to play with his girlfriend, Ruby. He looked up, and he saw me, leaning against the car with my arms folded. His reaction was comical and dumbfounded. He must have been wondering what I was doing there.

I just smiled and held out my arms in a welcoming way. "Come on, Charlie, let's go home," I gently commanded.

He happily ran over to the car and got in, apparently forgetting why he'd set off in the first place. After that, he never wandered off the property again. Poor Ruby must have wondered what ever happened to her new admirer.

I have to admit that I did not pay as much attention to Charlie while Bailey was with us. As she grew older, Bailey was less able to roughhouse with Alan as she had developed hip dysplasia. This is a fairly common disease, especially in purebreds such as Labradors, German shepherds, Rottweilers, and other large breeds. It's caused by malformation of the ball and socket in the joint. The two don't properly meet and cause a grinding motion while the dog is walking.

Although this malformation is present at birth, the symptoms typically don't show up until later on in the dog's life. You will likely start noticing a difference in their gait. Over time, the condition progresses, and if the dog lives long enough, it can become crippled.

I think Bailey was confused by the change in Alan's interaction with her. Now, Alan was exclusively roughhousing with Charlie, who loved every minute of it!

During this time, Alan and I noticed a neighbor's young golden retriever who was often on a long lead tied to a tree in the front yard. It didn't matter what time of day or evening we passed by that house, the poor guy was out there, sometimes while the kids ignored him as they busily played, but he was often alone. On one such day as we drove past their house, Alan had an idea.

"I was thinking," Alan said, "since Bailey is getting too old to play with Charlie, perhaps it's a good idea to approach our neighbors about taking their dog along on our hikes."

Naturally, I was nominated to make the first inquiry. Luckily, the mother, Nicole, was home when I knocked on the front door. At first, Nicole was taken aback by my request. But given she had a house full of kids, she quickly warmed up to the idea of someone taking the dog off her hands. With that, we started taking this timid yet spunky one-and-a-half-year-old golden retriever named Sparky on hikes regularly.

Interestingly, Charlie and Bailey didn't know what to make of their new friend when we first introduced them in our backyard. Of course, this shouldn't have been a surprise, because they were likely trying to figure out how this was going to impact the "pecking order" within the pack. But Sparky assumed a submissive posture, almost crawling toward us while simultaneously peeing. This behavior right away signaled to our two guys that Sparky was going to be the lowest ranking member of the pack.

Over time, we worked on Sparky's confidence. We didn't change the pack hierarchy, but we made him feel confident enough so that he didn't grovel or submissively pee in our or our dogs' presence. We did this by simply interacting with him. Sparky was never left out of any activity or form of affection we gave Bailey or Charlie.

Having Sparky hang out with us—taking him for hikes, paying special attention by brushing him, or giving him a treat—signaled to Sparky that he was an important member of the pack. As a result, Sparky became as bold as to try to initiate play with Charlie on many occasions, but all Charlie did was growl and scold poor Sparky. Our rationale for including Sparky in the pack so Charlie had a younger dog to play with wasn't going to plan. But this did not sway us one bit.

We continued to include Sparky regularly in our outings until his family abruptly put a stop to it. Nicole left a note at their front door one day when I went to go pick up Sparky for a walk. It informed me not to come and get him anymore. We weren't quite sure why this had happened. We were heartbroken, as we had grown attached to this lively, comical pooch.

He had always made Alan and I laugh with his goofy antics. Much of this was caused by Sparky's awkward approach to the world that had been kept from him.

Not long after Sparky was taken out of our lives, life for Bailey was to change.

About nine months earlier in mid-March, a few days before we were to leave for our road trip to New Mexico and the surrounding Southwest area, I had taken Bailey to the vet to get one of her routine vaccinations. The vet tech, Lynn, noticed that Bailey looked rather thin.

When we put Bailey on the scale, we saw she had lost almost ten pounds since her last visit only six months before. This was very concerning since Bailey lost this weight without being on a diet and while eating her usual amount of food everyday.

"Why don't you take Bailey into exam room two, and I will have Doctor Bennett come in and take a look at her," Lynn said as an expression of concern crossed her face.

As we waited, I began to look at Bailey more objectively. That is when I noticed how old she looked,

Last Dog

tired and yes, very thin. I felt awful; how could Alan and I have not noticed she wasn't well? We were so distracted by his restaurant opening and the hectic pace of my freelance schedule that we weren't paying attention. All that time, Bailey was suffering.

"Well, Miss Bailey, what is going on with you?" Karen asked in her usual playful tone as she walked in without really seeing Bailey yet.

Karen's demeanor changed when she got a look at her. She quickly consulted the latest notes in Bailey's chart that Lynn had just entered. Karen became very focused, kneeling down to where Bailey was sitting.

"Come on, old girl. Let's get up, so I can have a good look at you." Karen reflexively gave Bailey one of those dehydrated liver treats they always kept in a dog-shaped, ceramic container on the counter. Bailey obligingly wagged her tail.

Karen started feeling Bailey's body up and down, almost immediately stopping at mid-abdomen.

"I want to get her in immediately for an x-ray," Karen directed.

"What is it?" I blurted.

"She has an enlarged spleen," Karen said as she quickly escorted Bailey out for the exam room to get her x-ray.

I followed slowly while trying to process what I just heard.

Lynn and the vet tech staff didn't bother anesthetizing Bailey for the x-ray. They explained to me that they only needed a quick image, and it didn't have to be perfect to confirm Karen's manual diagnosis.

Once they had Bailey on the table for her x-ray, I returned to the exam room, expecting a long wait.

Instead, Karen returned rather quickly, without Bailey, tossed the x-ray film up on the light box, and showed me the huge mass that was in Bailey's abdomen. It was, as suspected, her spleen.

"It's about two-and-a-half times the size of what a normal spleen should be, and this is about to burst. I need to get her into surgery now," Karen said in the most urgent tone.

I hesitated a moment as I was trying to process the suddenness of it all.

"Of course, but will she be well enough to take this trip with us? We had planned to leave the day after tomorrow," I asked, almost sure that the answer was going to be no.

"She's a strong girl and should start feeling good pretty quickly once I remove her spleen. But I wouldn't take her on any hikes for at least a week. Better to ease her back into it with short walks. I want to keep her overnight for observation after the surgery, and then you can come and pick her up tomorrow," Karen said quickly as she rushed out of the exam room to prepare for surgery.

While still sitting in exam room two, I called Alan, who was in Hoboken, New Jersey, finishing things up at work before leaving for our three-week road trip.

"What's up? I am really busy; can I call you back later?" Alan said without me getting in a word.

"No, you can't," I sternly answered. "I am at the vet and Bailey is going into surgery."

"What! What are you talking about? What happened? I thought she was just going in to get vaccinated?"

I told Alan the incredible turn of events. He

couldn't believe it, almost to the point of challenging the diagnosis until I shared that I had seen the x-ray myself and that this was real. After calming down, Alan did admit that he had noticed lately that Bailey was looking thin and tired.

"Okay, I should be wrapping it up here soon, and I will head straight home. I hope we can still make this trip," Alan said.

My mind wondered to more urgent matters like, *I hope Bailey makes it through surgery.*

As Karen predicted, Bailey bounced back quickly, and by the time we arrived in Tucson, Arizona, she had recovered from surgery and was ready to go hiking. Bailey had that old spring in her step, and she was putting weight back on quickly, thanks to her big appetite!

Surgery bought Bailey an additional eight months of fun and adventure. Although we had been warned by Karen that though the biopsy from the spleen was inconclusive, there was a chance that it was cancer. If so, it would return to another organ.

Karen was right. We started to notice Bailey slowing down later that autumn. At Karen's recommendation, we took Bailey to a specialist in Albany, New York, who confirmed our suspicions. It was cancer, and it had spread to Bailey's liver and kidneys. She didn't have long since chemotherapy was not an option and never was for what was diagnosed by Karen as hemangiosarcoma. This is a cancer arising from the blood vessels.

Although I was preparing for the worse during those months following surgery, I still couldn't believe it. As we walked out of the clinic, I saw a four-month-old chocolate Labrador puppy, playfully bouncing around in the reception area. That is when I lost it and ran outside to collect myself. I was envisioning Bailey at that age, an age I never got to see but could only imagine, and now, she had so little time left. How fast it all goes by.

Bailey passed away a little over a month later, just after the New Year, at home in the very early morning hours on January 6, Little Christmas.

I will always remember her idiosyncrasies such as frantically licking my sweaty legs and arms after I returned from a run.

She'd follow me upstairs, waiting patiently while I peeled off my perspiration-soaked clothes so she could pick up the freshest and stinkiest item and proudly prance around the room with it. Even while I was doing laundry, Bailey was at the ready, sticking her nose into the basket of dirty clothes, hunting for the ripest item she could sniff out.

What I do miss the most about Bailey was her intuitiveness. One of our pet sitters, Cindy, pointed this out to us. She said it was rare for a dog to be so in-tuned. Bailey would know how to read your mood, and she'd always respond accordingly. Whenever my mood was low, like when we lost Ralf, she knew that all I needed was for her to sit quietly by my side. An occasional snuggle for reassurance perhaps, but she never pushed to be petted or played with.

Charlie and Bailey at Awosting.

Sparky (far left) enjoying being one of the pack.

CHAPTER 5: CHARLIE AND ABBY

Look Who Is Top Dog Now

Charlie and Abby, awaiting a handout during a hiking break.

Both Alan and I were saddened by Bailey's passing. But because she had been ailing for some time, we had known her death was imminent. We had prepared as much as we could emotionally. But for Charlie, that was another story.

We were surprised by the extent of his mourning. He would let out long, loud sighs while laying about the house. Whenever we took him for a hike, he would dash out of the car upon arrival and start darting around like he was trying to find someone. That someone must have been Bailey. When Charlie realized she was not there to greet him, his hopeful mood melted into disappointment.

Last Dog

This would happen even if we were visiting a friend's house or when we went to our apartment down near New York City. Charlie would gallop in, thinking he'd finally see his pal. Alan and I felt so bad for the guy. If it were up to us, we would have returned to a one-dog household with just Charlie. But our hearts broke each time Charlie's hopes were dashed.

Actually, Charlie's reaction was somewhat surprising, because he and Bailey had seldom played together. I guess their companionship on walks, at playgroup, while sleeping, and the occasional tug-of-war session had been enough to make Charlie miss Bailey something awful.

"I can't stand this anymore," I said to Alan one morning over breakfast. "I can't even take time to mourn the loss of Bailey, because Charlie is breaking my heart. I hate to say it, but I think we need to get another dog."

In retrospect, we should have waited longer, because most dogs do get over loss. I suspect if we had waited about three months, Charlie would have bounced back. But the four weeks we had waited since Bailey's passing seemed like an eternity. So, we started looking online for a female Labrador to rescue.

There she was, Miss Abigail, romping around on an online video. Like Bailey, she was also a chocolate Labrador and was about-seven-and-a-half years old. She looked and acted like a pup, full of energy in the video, running around with a stuffed toy. The off-camera voice called it her "baby." She was being fostered by a family in southern Massachusetts, which was about a two-hour ride from our home.

She resembled Bailey, which was surprising

because Bailey was not a typical-looking chocolate Labrador. We were told by vets and others familiar with the breed that Bailey looked like she had some Chesapeake Bay retriever in her background or perhaps she was an English Labrador. We made a few phone calls, and before I knew it, the three of us were in a car, heading to meet Abby.

It was early February when we picked Abby up. We met the foster family who had a house filled with rescue dogs, a few from Hurricane Katrina. Abby was the most rambunctious of the dogs, running around the house, excited by our visit in a way similar to how Bailey had been when we'd first met her.

Charlie was super calm in the backyard enclosure as he and Abby got acquainted. He seemed nonplussed by Abby. I think her energy had the opposite effect on him and made Charlie even mellower, almost indifferent. I felt like saying to Charlie, "You know we are doing this for you, fella!"

After a long conversation with the foster family and the adoption counselor, we got the all clear to take Abby home with us. In a way, we felt bad because she had been with this family for several months, and she had developed a bond with them and the other dogs.

There was one dog in particular named China, who she had chased around the house during most of our visit. They were as "thick as thieves." It turned out they were rescued together, so who knew how far their friendship went back.

The foster family told us Abby enjoyed sitting on the recliner sofa with them while they ate dinner and watched TV. Alan and I exchanged a look. If there had been a bubble over our heads, it would have read, *Well,*

Last Dog

we're putting an end to that! Luckily, our furniture did not include a recliner sofa.

Cheryl, the woman fostering Abby, shared, "Abby loves her stuffed toys, which we named her 'babies.' When you want her to get her toy, all you have to say is, 'Abby, go get your baby,' and she'll immediately retrieve one of them for you."

Well, that sounded cute enough.

 LEARNING: While Abby's foster family thought it was adorable that she sat on the recliner chair with them while they ate dinner and watched TV, it was actually an invasion of their space. This would not be tolerated in the wolf pack where each member is respectful of the other's space.

Just think of a pack member trying to get in on a fresh kill of the alpha and/or beta wolf. I don't think that habit would last too long. That member would be severely punished, and if it persisted, they'd be cast out of the pack or even killed.

When your dog jumps up on your lap without being prompted or jumps up on you, it is a sign they are not respecting your status in the pack. It is not as brazen and aggressive as Hunter mounting me, but nonetheless, the act is less about them showing you affection and more about them asserting themselves within the pack.

WE PRESSED to make our exit as a long drive lay ahead of us, and the light was starting to fade on this mid-winter's day. It wasn't easy getting out of the house without Abby's friend, China, trying to follow.

But we managed.

I exited first with Charlie and got him into the car. There I sat, waiting for Alan to emerge. He did after awhile with Abby pulling him, which was especially dangerous since much of their driveway was a sheet of ice. I could see the look on Alan's face, and it was not good.

"I was tempted to turn around and take her back into the house and tell them she wasn't the right dog for us. I could tell that she was going to be a handful to train," he later told me.

Alan turned out to be right. Abby was the most out-of-control dog we had ever adopted, and she lacked much of the training you'd expect for a dog her age to have. I guess this was *the* reason why she had been passed from one household to the next for the past seven-and-a-half years. We were her fifth home. She had never gotten the discipline and training needed to make her behave as an adult dog should. But Abby was going to get the training she long needed, and it was going to start tomorrow whether she liked it or not!

Abby behaved well during the car ride home, but she panted non-stop for the entire two hours. There was never a momentary lull just to catch her breath. We thought she was thirsty, so we pulled to the side of the road to give her water we had in the car. But she wasn't interested. Poor Charlie was trying to catch some ZZZs in the back but couldn't because of her incessant panting. We were soon to discover that this was Abby's M.O. She was an excitable dog that knew no speeds other than zero and ninety.

It also didn't help that Abby's medium frame weighed-in at about eighty-five pounds, which was

Last Dog

overweight for her. So obviously, we needed to put Missy, as I affectionately called her, on a diet.

As Abby had pulled Alan toward our car the day we adopted her, she had unknowingly signed up for doggie boot camp.

Abby had to quickly adapt to a strict diet program and learn a new way to behave in the house. The poor girl, she didn't know what had hit her. She must have been thinking, *What's up with this? I can't sit on your lap while you're eating dinner? I can't sit on any piece of furniture I like? I can't be petted twenty-four seven?*

We did not pull any punches. The word "no'" was said to her a lot in those first six months, and she did not like it. And she persisted in trying to get her way. It was as if we had to break her, like a bronco posing as a Labrador. This seven-and-a-half-year-old possessed boundless energy. We checked her paper work several times to make sure her age was correctly stated.

That winter, we had lots and lots of snow. It just kept piling up. The far end of our backyard was traversed only by us and the wildlife that passed through, so much of it was knee-deep, virgin snow. It became part of our hiking routine to put Abby out in front so she could act as our snowplow, making a path for the three of us.

This was especially helpful to Charlie, since he was in the early stages of elbow dysplasia, which was slowing him down. He got the benefit of traveling along a fairly well-worn path thanks to Abby and us. Charlie was perfectly fine with bringing up the rear.

But we found that even a two-hour walk in virgin snow was not enough to turn Abby's switch off at night. Shortly upon our return, she was up for a game of tug-of-war. At first, Charlie would oblige, but then he'd run out of gas and curl up on his bed. Then it was our turn to tucker her out, but Abby's energy reserves seemed endless. Alan and I were exhausted after an evening with our "Energizer doggie." She just kept going and going.

"Are you sure you are looking at her paperwork correctly? She can't be this old," Alan challenged. "Charlie is just a year older than Abby, and he is as fit as a fiddle. But even he has to take a nap at some point in the day."

"I know. Where is the off switch?" I exclaimed.

We had thought we'd had it down to a science with Bailey, who had a lot of energy when she was young. We knew how to get an energetic dog to a state of what we'd call "broken ass." That's when our dogs were so exhausted from the day's activities that they'd just pass out. It didn't matter if you came out with something yummy to eat; in this state, nothing mattered. They were not budging!

But we couldn't seem to achieve this state of exhaustion with Abby. What to do? Then an idea hatched from advice we had gotten.

Karen had said, "Abby is a breed of working dog. Give her a job. Put a backpack on her and load it with bottles of water. This will instill a sense of purpose while she is hiking and should help tire her out."

So we did this. But soon, water bottles were replaced with something even heavier—four cans of beans on each side. Let's just say we saw a difference. Not exactly "broken ass" but her pilot light went out a bit earlier on those evenings.

We achieved several goals with this approach. We

Last Dog

tired Abby out sooner, knocked the weight off her more quickly, and got her into shape in time for spring. Abby had slimmed down to sixty-three pounds by the time June came around. She had developed muscle tone, the result of hiking through snowdrifts with cans of beans in her backpack. Abby didn't mind any of it. In fact, she thought it was fun. Her super-positive disposition made boot camp all the easier for everyone involved.

By the time spring rolled around, Abby was trained to walk off-leash, although it was a constant battle at first to get her to walk behind us or at least behind Alan. Abby always wanted to be out in front.

It was easier than we thought it would be with her. We used the same method as we did with all our dogs, which was a gradual weaning off the leash. We'd used a much longer leash than usual for this training, so that the leash would drag on the ground within a comfortable distance from our feet so that we could quickly stop or slow down our dogs' gait with a matching word command. They would eventually associate the command with what was physically expected of them.

For Abby, this took a little bit longer, but she finally got it. The training was complete when the use of a leash was no longer needed, and they responded to our verbal commands just as quickly. The commands functioned as a mental leash that allowed our dogs, and us, to more fully enjoy their walks and hikes.

Abby was the official greeter, acting as if it were her duty to say hello to everyone we passed on our walks—people first, then their dogs. Basically, the people didn't have a choice, especially if Abby had it in mind to say hello and eke out a petting or two. For the most part, it worked out okay. On those rare occasions when a passerby ignored her, Abby would turn to us with a perplexed look.

"How could anyone *not* want to say hello to you!" was our usual, light-hearted response to her confused reaction.

Although Abby's gregariousness was adorable, we knew it wasn't proper to allow her to barrel ahead and defy our commands. So Alan took to walking Abby with a herding stick. It was simply a long, staff-like stick that he could use to keep her behind him if she decided to try to pass on one side or the other.

"She's coming up on your left," I would warn.

The stick acted as a barrier of sorts, reminding her to stay behind the alpha. After awhile, just the gesture of Alan holding out the herding stick kept her from charging ahead. It became a mental barrier.

But sometimes, that mental barrier could not stand up to extraordinary temptation. I recall two occasions when this became dangerous. Once was when Alan was walking Abby and Charlie off-leash at one of our favorite and familiar trails.

A woman was walking her boxer off-leash, too. Abby was straining to get around Alan to go over and say hello.

"Is your dog friendly?" Alan yelled over to the woman.

But it was a moot point, because Abby managed to get by Alan and made a dash toward both the dog and woman.

"I don't know," the woman responded nervously just before her dog clamped its mouth on Abby's head, making several puncture wounds. One of them was

Last Dog

dangerously close to her eye.

Alan managed to disengage her dog from Abby and get her on-leash. The woman seemed startled by it all.

Charlie wisely stayed behind during this entire scene. He was pretty good at picking up other dog's vibes where Abby was clueless!

The other incident occurred when I was hiking with Abby and Charlie in the Shawangunks on a backcountry trail with lots of rocky outcrops. Charlie was taking his sweet time, sniffing and investigating, while Abby rushed ahead as if she was late for something. I caught up to Abby and turned for no more than a second to check on Charlie when I heard a rattling sound.

I turned around to see Abby investigating the edge of a rock outcrop where a timber rattlesnake lay. It had its head raised up pretty high from where it had been resting. I thought it could have been a female, feeling threatened as she protected her nest.

Unfortunately, the rattle sound did not faze Abby. She had no reason to know that was a warning. She stood within a snout's length of this agitated and ready-to-strike snake. I wasted no time and grabbed Abby's tail, and I flung her in the opposite direction. Adrenaline must have given me the strength to lift Abby off the ground and send her into flight.

She was unhurt but a little shaken. I immediately leashed her and Charlie, who came walking onto the scene, thankfully late to the party. We quickly passed by that spot and walked several yards before my legs gave out, and I was forced to sit to regain my composure. I was shaking like a leaf.

Despite our early struggles with training Abby to walk properly off-leash, I did eventually manage to train her to respond to several verbal commands on our walks. Abby didn't need to be facing me when I gave a command such as "slow down" or "stop" or "out" for when she had her nose in something she shouldn't.

Sometimes, I would include a loud clap or two to get her to turn her attention toward me. If she was lagging behind or had wandered too far from my right or left, I would simply slap the side of my hip and say, "stay with me." Abby would happily close the gap between us.

As Abby grew older and her hearing was not as good as it used to be, I started to introduce hand signals to accompany the already-familiar verbal commands.

Another great training method that proved to be lots of fun for Abby and Charlie was what we called, "sit-stay-release." Alan did this training using our front and backyard. Alan would start by grabbing a handful of treats and command Abby and Charlie to sit. Abby, of course, wiggled with great anticipation. Charlie was a pro, sitting patiently still.

Alan would slowly back away from them while repeatedly saying, "stay," and both of them would stay.

As he backed away, I'd start to hear low, whiny sounds coming from both of them. I could see their anticipation grow as they struggled to remain in the sitting position. The farther Alan moved away, the more difficult it was for them to remain sitting still, even for a pro like Charlie.

If one of them started to stand, Alan would course correct immediately with a stern sit. If this didn't work, and it was usually Abby who had difficulty complying,

Last Dog

Alan would walk back toward them and command her to sit. After a few tries, she'd obey. Then the process would start all over again.

Eventually, Abby and Charlie got so good at this that Alan could walk over to the other side of the house, out of their sight, but they'd still sit until they heard him yell, "Okay, c'mon, guys."

With that, they bolted, making a mad dash to wherever Alan was to rightfully collect their treat.

What Abby and Charlie learned in this training was so helpful. If they were following one of us down our driveway to put out or retrieve the trash bins, all we had to do was make a verbal or a hand command, and they'd sit and stay until we returned. Another great benefit of this training was that it got them to heel to our command even if we weren't in their sight. This is usually not the case for many dogs. Often dogs will not heel to a command unless their guardian is standing in front of them.

The relationship Charlie had with Abby was quite different from the one he'd had with Bailey. Charlie was top dog now, but he didn't achieve this all on his own. Since Abby was pushy, we had to insert ourselves to make sure she adhered to the pecking order. To accomplish this, we did things like making sure Charlie got in and out of the car and went into the house first. Alan showed preference toward Charlie so Abby would get the message. I was the beta in our pack.

A beta is the second in command who not only steps into the role when the alpha is away but also the one to provide support and care to the other pack mates. My role was to help Abby ease into the pack. Our influence on our pack's hierarchy also seemed to spill over into the Dog Love playgroup pack.

"You know, ever since you got Abby, Charlie's now mounting the other dogs in playgroup," Emily, the owner of the playgroup said with a chuckle as she remembered it wasn't too long ago when it was the other way around for Charlie.

Charlie had grown into his own. With Bailey gone from our pack, Charlie felt more comfortable to assume this position. We may have taken things too far as Charlie started to make a habit of mounting Abby. It was usually after dinner when Abby would settle down to play with one of her woobies. Charlie would purposely take it away from Abby. If she'd grab another, he'd take that one, too. If she got up, he would mount her. That's when it became time for one of us to play referee, reprimanding Charlie and returning the woobie to Abby. We had to dial the "top dog" thing back a bit.

LEARNING: As is true with children, if you give a dog an inch they will take a yard, or in Abby's case, a mile. Giving your dog leeway even once is something they will remember. Given the next chance, they will try to assert themselves even more. Regardless of the dog's disposition, they are all opportunists. This is not a slight against dogs. Their survival instinct drives this behavior. If given the chance, dogs will try to assume more of a leadership position in the pack.

So be warned if you are thinking, *oh, just this one time, I will let them up on the couch or the bed or eat out of my plate*. I can guarantee you that your dogs are not thinking the way you are!

Last Dog

I DON'T want you to think Charlie was a bully. He wasn't. Charlie was a mild-mannered, mellow-yellow Labrador. That's what I liked to call him, my "mellow-yellow." But as he got older, I called him, "my old man" and sometimes "cranky pants" when he'd make grumbling noises, voicing his discontent about failing to get walked or fed on time.

Charlie had blossomed into quite a character. You wouldn't know it upon meeting him or even if you stayed over a few days, because Charlie only felt comfortable with showing his true self with us and certain extended family members. Alan was best in bringing this out in Charlie, and I'm glad he did. It was a way for Charlie to express himself and have fun at the same time.

Alan loves games, and I have to say he knows how to get down to a dog's level. He knows how to make the simplest things—like going for a walk, playing woobies, sitting in the backyard, or feeding time—a lot of fun.

Our walks in the country should have been stimulating enough with an array of smells, animal life sightings, or swimming. But Alan sprinkled in added excitement by pointing out wildlife scat, paw prints, and chipmunk and ground hog holes with a sense of urgency that got our guys going.

In a high whisper, Alan would say to Charlie, "What's that?" He'd point to a spot on the ground.

Charlie would come charging over in great anticipation of the next find. Sometimes, Alan's finds failed to illicit much interest other than a quick sniff, but other times, it was like he'd hit the jackpot! Charlie would smell the spot frantically and then the surrounding area like a police dog. If it was really a good find, he'd start darting in different directions in pursuit of the scent's owner. Sometimes, Abby would catch on and do the same. The two of them would inevitably knock into each other in all the excitement. I wish I had a video of that!

Back home, the fun didn't end. When sitting in the backyard, Alan would suddenly get up, usually while Charlie was napping, and yell, "Charge," as he ran toward the garden fence where the chipmunks would often be hanging out. Charlie would bolt out of a deep sleep and be right behind Alan, bringing up the rear, following him closely in hopes of bagging a chipmunk.

Luckily, this didn't happen. Those little guys are so fast and have such a network of escape routes that they'd disappear in an instant, leaving Charlie perplexed. Although they escaped, I am sure the chipmunks didn't appreciate the sport. I came to calling these play sessions, "Charlie and the Chipmunks."

Once dinnertime approached, Charlie had a habit of staring me down. If I was around, I was the one who fed them. As six p.m. approached, I could feel Charlie's stare. I'd turn to him, and his coal-colored eyes were like a laser on me. If I moved in the slightest, he would get up in anticipation. If I got up for any reason, he'd follow me closely.

Charlie usually won, wearing down my resistance to the point that there were many occasions when he and Abby ate before six p.m., especially in the winter. I used to joke that Charlie had a clock in his belly and it never adjusted to the lack of Daylight Saving time.

In the spring and summer, our dogs were pretty much outside dogs. They went outside right after

Last Dog

breakfast, took a quick trip inside the house for dinner, and went back outside until dusk. I think Charlie's favorite time of day was late afternoon, especially in the summertime.

He'd lay in the backyard, soaking up the late day sun as he took a nap. I'm sure the sounds of the birds and other wildlife lulled him to sleep. I'd hear him snore and see parts of his body twitch or his paws move in a running motion as he went into dream land. Alan called it "Azoyga" land. I'm not sure where he got that name from. But something inside Charlie would inevitably wake him up just around feeding time. Darn that clock in his belly!

After the dogs were fed, Alan would initiate some indoor play, especially during the winter months. Since Charlie and Abby were pretty much outside dogs, it was a difficult transition for them and us as the days grew shorter. On these long, winter evenings, they were inside the house starting in the late afternoon. So Alan managed to continue the fun and games inside the house and took woobie-play to a whole new level.

It would start out as a tug-of-war, but if Alan won that round, he'd get up and run away from Charlie with the woobie in hand. Charlie was always in hot pursuit as they made their way into the kitchen.

Our kitchen layout was perfect for a game of chase, because Charlie could run through it and the adjacent laundry room in a continuous circle. And this is exactly what they did while I was cooking—how convenient!

It was comical. One moment, Alan was being chased by Charlie, and in the next, Alan would be chasing Charlie, who had the woobie in his mouth.

Over time, Charlie figured out how to fake out

Alan. He'd stand still, waiting for Alan to take off in either direction before moving in the opposite direction. He'd peer around corners to see where Alan was. In return, Alan would play unfairly by opening the pantry or refrigerator door, stopping Charlie in his tracks as Alan tauntingly called, "Charlie, Charlie."

I don't think I am anthropomorphizing when I describe Charlie as extremely frustrated and angry whenever Alan played unfairly, because he'd start barking incessantly, making his feelings made clear as if saying, "Hey, not fair, dude!"

And while this ruckus was going on, Abby was happily sitting on her bed in the living room, left alone to chew on her woobie and enjoying a brief reprieve from Charlie's usual harassment. Ultimately, I'd have to be the bad guy and bring this enjoyable game of chase to an end. It posed a challenge during cooking that *I* wasn't game for.

When it came to *our* dinnertime, Charlie was indeed a taskmaster. It started with Charlie sitting beneath my feet while I cooked.

I would jokingly say to Charlie, "Are you here for your cooking class?" Of course, he was there for handouts, both intentional and accidental ones.

The longer it took for a meal to finish cooking, the less patience Charlie had. He couldn't wait for us to sit and have our meal so he could enjoy more handouts topped off with a half piece of cookie. Then Charlie's day was complete, and he could finally settle in for the night and go to sleep.

And sleep he did. I think he enjoyed his sleep as much as his walks. We'd swear that there was a smile on his face each night he turned in. One of us would say out aloud to him, "Another good day Charlie, eh?" Soon, the snoring and dream-induced twitching would follow, accompanied by an occasional yelp, growl, or tail wag. God only knows what he dreamt about, but it looked like he was enjoying it.

As Charlie grew older, his elbow dysplasia got worse. He was diagnosed with it at about seven years old, and by the time he reached twelve, his elbows had fused at a noticeably awkward angle. According to our vet, Karen, this was probably the best we could hope for.

"Since he has such good muscle tone, Charlie's shoulder muscles are now doing most of the work in getting him along on his hikes," Karen explained. "However, it's impressive that he's still hiking as much as he is."

Charlie hiked anywhere from a mile to three miles until he was just about to turn fourteen years old! We did just about everything to ease his dysplasia, including glucosamine supplements with MSM, Adequan injections, and cold laser therapy. The only thing we regretfully didn't try was acupuncture.

LEARNING: When Charlie was older and his elbow dysplasia was apparent, we had a few people suggest that we stop taking him for long walks, keeping his outings short or perhaps confined to the backyard.

I never considered that advice for a second. I think keeping Charlie active, despite his dysplasia, was what had made him able to continue to do as much as he did as he grew older. It kept him young not only in body but at heart, too. Charlie was most motivated to go for walks when it was at his favorite places.

Cynthia Flowers

So if he was feeling stiff, he was less willing to get up for a walk in our backyard. But if we were heading off our property to the orchard across the street or in the back—or better yet going for a ride in the car, which inevitably resulted in a walk—nothing could hold Charlie back.

What I learned from this is to not prematurely age your dog. If they are up for it and want to do it, then let them continue to channel their inner puppy.

IF I DON'T remember everything that made Charlie who he was, I *will* remember he was always up for fun even as he got older. He *loved* his walks, playing woobies with Alan, and playfully picking on Abby.

He enjoyed being the elder statesman of the playgroup he attended even up until the week of his passing. While Bailey had the distinction of being among the first dogs to attend the playgroup, Charlie was one of the playgroup's oldest and longest-attending dogs.

Charlie would make a stink every time the playgroup van arrived. As he lay on the deck, enjoying the early morning sun's warmth, he'd suddenly get up and start barking because he could hear the van bouncing up the road and turning down our driveway. He would bark as he walked toward the van and got in. I'm not sure if he was trying to re-establish his position in this pack or if he was just saying hello.

Oddly, once inside the van, Charlie grew quiet and well behaved as the van went on its way. As old as he was, Charlie always wanted to go to playgroup or out for walks, regardless of the weather. A little rain or snow and we'd just put on his rain jacket, and he was

Last Dog

good to go.

Charlie passed away after a short illness just as he turned fourteen years old. He had central vestibular disease, which is usually terminal. The best way to describe it is like having constant vertigo where he couldn't get up from a lying position. It happened on Christmas Eve night, and poor Charlie was like this for five days, never showing much of an improvement.

He'd had a vestibular episode about ten months earlier when he just turned thirteen. At first, I hadn't known what was going on with him as he'd walked drunkenly to his bowl for breakfast. He had trouble picking up the kibble from his bowl and standing steadily. My first thought was he'd had a stroke.

After I had gotten him fed and settled, I consulted the internet and learned that it was more likely vestibular disease, which often strikes old dogs. It's fittingly called "Old Dog Vestibular." The vestibular is a vein located in the inner ear. Depending on how severely this vein is affected, your dog could have a mild or severe attack. Luckily, Charlie's first event was not severe but enough to affect his balance for a couple of days.

After evaluating Charlie's symptoms from this first episode, Karen had warned that he would likely have another before the year was out, and it would probably be worse. Unfortunately, like everything she had told us over the years, Karen had been right. The next episode Charlie had was ten months later.

It was Christmas Eve, and we were visiting Alan's mother. It was a full house of visitors in and out that day. Charlie and Abby were enjoying themselves. After we had our dinner, I went into the kitchen to feed them.

Cynthia Flowers

They rushed to their food bowls as if they were starving despite getting their fair share of handouts all day. Charlie finished first and was following me out of the kitchen until my detour into the bathroom.

No sooner than I had gotten inside to lock the door and flick on the light, I heard Alan yell and his sister, Janis, cry out, "What's wrong with him?"

I bolted out of the bathroom to see Charlie stretched out on his side on the living room floor. His eyes were shut, and his entire body was vibrating.

These bouts came and went during the evening. We were too afraid to move him. We ended up sleeping in the living room to wait it out with Charlie.

But once morning came and we saw he wasn't getting better, we decided to cancel Christmas Day plans at my parents on Long Island, New York and take Charlie to the emergency animal hospital near our home in Upstate New York.

Once our vet's office opened the day after Christmas, we moved Charlie from the emergency hospital where it had been confirmed that he was having a vestibular event. Whether Charlie was experiencing a central or a peripheral event couldn't be confirmed just yet, the difference being a central event usually comes with a terminal diagnosis.

"It looks like he is having a central vestibular event this time. Charlie's eyes are moving in a circular rather than a left-to-right motion," Karen said apologetically.

We didn't give up right away and kept him at the vet overnight for further observation. Charlie improved to the point of sitting upright instead of lying on his side with his eyes shut. So we were hopeful.

As we made our way to the back room of the vet's

office where Charlie was resting in a kennel, Karen told us, "I gave Charlie a good talking-to this morning and told him as a Christmas gift to you both he just has to pull through."

We were so happy to see Charlie in better spirits, and he was happy to see us, too. He made motions as if he was going to get up, but it didn't amount to much more of an effort then or at any other time, unfortunately.

The one day we had Charlie at home after taking him back from the vet's office, he sat on his bed on the back deck to enjoy the sun like he always did. Then he sat with us in the living room on the same bed until the evening when another vestibular event hit while he was sleeping.

The poor guy was having a really rough time as his head moved in a swirling motion whenever he tried to lift it up from the bed. He yelped and cried. It broke our hearts. I hugged him repeatedly, but it didn't seem to help.

The poor guy didn't know what was happening. His world must have been spinning before his eyes. Closing his eyes didn't make it much better, either. We rushed Charlie back to the emergency clinic where they gave him a heavy sedative that allowed him to sleep.

The vet on call that night informed us rather matter-of-factly, "He's having a severe central vestibular event. Since he's been like this for several days with very little improvement and is experiencing another one, the prognosis is not good. We recommend that you put him to sleep."

After much angst and back-and-forth debating, Alan agreed to let Charlie go. We were given a few moments privacy to sit with Charlie while he slept, snoring as usual. That put a smile on our faces, ever so briefly. I stroked his smooth, soft, yellow coat several times and told him how much I loved him. Alan broke down uncontrollably, sobbing as he held Charlie for what would be the last time. I clipped some of his fur as a memento, and then we left as Charlie was wheeled away.

Everyone who had anything to do with Charlie missed him big time when he was gone. While we were given little time to emotionally prepare for his eminent passing, it was the best for Charlie. He'd been able to live every day the way he wanted. Just two days before he'd become acutely ill, he had joined me and Abby on a three-mile hike on a sunny, crispy-cold December day. Less than a week later, he was gone. Charlie truly enjoyed life to the fullest and to the very end!

Charlie strikes a perfect pose.

CHAPTER 6: ABIGAIL

Last and Loving It

Abby cooling off at Black Creek.

Abigail found herself to be the last surviving dog in our family. We didn't give into the impulse to find her a companion once Charlie had passed away. This was partly because her mourning period was not as intense and was shorter.

And quite frankly, I'm not sure Abby truly mourned Charlie's passing. It was more like she was confused. She'd look around for him on a hike, the house, outside in the yard in the direction where Charlie would usually sit or wander as though she were expecting him to appear. Secretly, so were Alan and I.

We held our breath, hoping that Abby's

"mourning" would be no worse than this and would finally fade away. We were holding firm on not adopting another dog. We had always planned to take a short break from having dogs, and we saw this as the right time to make this happen.

"We have to remain strong," I kept saying to Alan. "If this is the worst it gets with her, then we should be okay."

Despite our challenging work schedules, we made sure Abby was kept busy, perhaps too busy, for a thirteen-year-old. We continued to send her to playgroup twice a week so she'd get her fix of dog interaction. Alan's brother, John, was only working part-time at his job and would come occasionally for day visits to take her for hikes. And quite unexpectedly, Alan lavished Abby with some overdue attention and love.

It was remarkable to watch the relationship between Alan and Abby evolve. She went from the lower-ranking pack member, who was constantly disciplined by Alan and wanting of his affection, to the top dog who finally enjoyed Alan's full acceptance and affection. This made Abby the happiest pooch in the world. She was simply "over the moon."

Surprisingly, Abby was the tonic for Alan's profound loss. He mourned Charlie like he'd mourned no other loss in his life. After he went through the deepest depths of his grief, he found the ability to channel the love he had for Charlie to Abby. This was the best thing that could have happened to them both.

"Hey there little girl," Alan would say in a high-pitched, playful voice as he greeted Abby in the morning.

Last Dog

And not only would Abby's tail wag, but her whole body would, too. She was beyond happy. She'd press into him, looking up fondly as Alan gave her a vigorous petting and hugs. He was her new best friend. Since I was away from home more, traveling for work, and Alan was able to do a good amount of his work from home, the bond between the two of them grew exponentially. They went everywhere together. He'd work downstairs in the kitchen so she wouldn't be sitting by herself. It was a beautiful thing to see, Alan finally accepting Abby for the dog she was, not longing for the one he wanted her to be.

LEARNING: Alan would say to me many times over the years that I needed to be more consistent in disciplining our dogs. These acts were as simple as me forgetting and letting the dog walk out the door in front of me or failing to keep them from running ahead of me when on a walk. Letting these acts go by once would be remembered by our dogs.

Consistency is essential. Basically, your dogs want to please you, and it's your job to let them know how. Consistency will better ensure the behavior will become second nature to your dog. The formula that has worked best for us is a combination of discipline, exercise and love—in that order.

Of course, this is easier said than done, and by no means were we perfect at it. But once we got into a groove, we saw the results, and it made our lives and our dogs' lives so much easier. Whether we were at home, visiting, or traveling, we could count on our dogs to be well behaved.

Cynthia Flowers

ABBY DID take on some new behaviors soon after Charlie had passed on. She began barking on occasion. Before this, we'd never heard her bark, not even a peep. We were convinced she didn't know how. The first time was when we had some landscapers in the backyard, pruning trees.

"Did you hear that? Was that Abby?" Alan asked in disbelief.

We both scooted out to the back deck to find Abby at the top of the stairs, barking in a deep, guttural tone at the landscapers. She actually sounded intimidating. I think Charlie would've been impressed; we certainly were.

"You know, that used to be Charlie's job," I remarked to Alan.

Maybe now she feels it's her job to be the watch dog?" he speculated.

"I thought she would have had a higher pitched bark than that," I went on to critique.

The next new behavior to come from Abby was in her vocalization to us. This wasn't barking exactly. It sounded similar to the sing-song noises Charlie used to make.

Charlie had been a master at this. We knew when he wanted to eat, when he was overdue for a walk, and when he was tired of sitting outside by himself and wanted us to join him.

For example, Alan and I would sit in the screened-in porch, which is close to the living room. However, it is difficult to get a straight view from the living room to the porch because the den is in between.

When Charlie was on his bed in the living room, he would give us a grace period of about five or ten

Last Dog

minutes before he'd start his high-pitched serenade. If that went ignored, his song would turn into a low woof of frustration and then return to serenading.

Alan and I would laugh as Charlie went through his entire repertoire before we'd let him and Abby join us on the porch. Mind you, this was a solo act; Abby was not singing backup.

But not too long after Charlie had passed on, during our dinner in the screened porch, we heard what sounded like Abby trying to recreate Charlie's "singing for dinner" routine. Alan and I looked at each other in mid-chew.

"That couldn't be Abby, could it?" I mumbled with a mouthful of food. "Maybe it's a coyote pup in the woods?"

Then we heard it again.

"No, that's Abby. What do you know, I guess she's figured out that now it's up to her to sing for *our* dinner," Alan said excitedly.

With that, we called her in. I may have imagined this, but Abby seemed happier than usual—if that was possible—as she rambled into the screened-in porch. Perhaps a sense of accomplishment fueled her mood!

The final incident that spooked us a bit was Abby licking both front legs up and down after snacking on one of her favorite food handouts. She had never done anything like this before

However, it had been a ritual of Charlie's. The more he liked something, the more thorough he was in getting the taste, scent, or both on his two front legs.

When we saw Abby do this, we said nothing but just looked at each other with a slight unease, thinking perhaps Abby was somehow "channeling" Charlie at that very moment!

LEARNING: In the wolf pack, if the alpha or the beta passes away, one of the other pack members will try to move up the ranks to assume this role. In our experience, this appeared to be true in our dog pack.

We saw Charlie do this after Bailey had passed away. Now that our pack was minus Charlie, there was an opportunity for Abby to expand her role by assuming some responsibilities. Charlie had been the one to alert us to "intruders" in our territory.

Now, Abby stepped up to the plate to do this job. She also became prescriptive about her feeding time and had picked up where Charlie left off in making me or Alan aware that it was nearing or past her feeding time. Abby had learned well from the master.

ABBY WAS a dog that was younger at heart than her years. Even when the disease of aging began to catch up with her, she pushed on. We had a couple of hurdles thrown our way with her. The first one happened when Abby turned twelve and she began experiencing seizures. We had never witnessed one before, and it scared the shit out of us.

We had no idea what to do. Could she swallow her tongue, have a heart attack, or die from it? This swam through my head during the thirty to forty-five seconds Abby was seizing on the living room floor with foam bubbling out of her mouth.

"What do we do? How do we get her to stop?" we both yelled simultaneously. To whom, I don't know, because we were both first timers at this.

Last Dog

We yelled at Abby, "Come out of it, sweetie. C'mon, Abby!" I tapped her several times to see if I could break the cycle.

Our shouts grew louder with desperation, and I was on the edge of getting hysterical. Just like that the seizing stopped. Abby became very still and quiet.

"Is she still breathing," Alan pleaded.

"Yes, yes," I answered in between catching my breath.

As we waited for Abby to come around, we called her name softly to avoid startling her and possibly causing another seizure.

After about a minute, Abby gradually opened her eyes and came back to us. Slowly, she picked up her head and looked around as if she had no idea what had hit her. After reading up on seizures later that night, she likely didn't know. We were told by Karen and later by a neurologist veterinarian that when dogs experience seizures, they're not aware of what's happening. I hope this is true.

However, soon after the seizure, Abby did experience what appeared to be disorientation, anxiety, excessive excitement, and a slight aggressiveness in her behavior. It wasn't threatening, but a bit of a departure from her usual self.

She would pace around the house for a couple hours, walking aimlessly as if trying to find something. She would stay close to one of us and follow wherever we went, even trying to join me in the bathroom, which is something she had never done previously.

Abby hadn't had a seizure in over a year. But one happened the week after Charlie passed away, so it was even more disheartening.

Damn, I thought we were out of the woods," Alan complained.

But we were disappointed further as the seizures came more frequently, sometimes only five days apart. We were forced to try Phenobarbital, which is considered a dirty drug because it has a lot of potential side effects. Abby was overly sensitive to anything sedating, so when she felt its effects coming on, she would whimper and cry.

I couldn't stand it, and she was not herself, very mopey and low energy. I was told that she would finally adjust to it, but it had been two weeks, and it didn't seem like that was happening at all. So we took her off the Phenobarbital and found a holistic supplement named Neuroplex that had several good reviews online.

She stopped having seizures all together for quite awhile. However, there was a non-serious, yet unpleasant side effect that Abby had experienced until her system got used to the contents in the supplement. It was gastrointestinal in nature.

"Well, at least she's not sedated, but man, she has been cutting some foul ones!" Alan complained.

"Better that than her being doped up or even worse, having weekly seizures," I defended.

And most importantly, Abby was herself. We had the best of both worlds at least for a while.

When the seizures did return after being on the holistic supplement for about year, Alan noticed that Abby's urine smelled unusually pungent.

"I noticed this smell all week when I'd let her out," Alan remarked. "Her urine doesn't usually smell this bad."

Last Dog

The best way to describe it was that her urine smelled very similar to overly ripe chicken broth.

"Yeah, you're right, this does smell different than usual," I agreed as I smelled the spot she had just went on in the backyard.

I took a specimen of Abby's urine to the vet's office the next morning only to get a phone call a few hours later from the vet tech, Lynn.

She delivered the color commentary. "This UTI is off the charts. We've never seen an infection that bad before."

"Lovely," I sarcastically retorted on the phone.

Karen prescribed mega doses of antibiotics for two weeks. But unfortunately, once Abby was off the antibiotics, the UTIs would return and so would the seizures. So back to the internet I went to discover that if someone has a disposition toward seizures, an infection could lower the threshold for more seizures.

"We need to make sure the UTIs don't return," I said to Alan.

"Well how do we do that? Keep her on antibiotics for the rest of her life?" Alan asked.

"You've got a point," I admitted.

When I returned to the vet for a follow-up, I shared my finding, and Karen agreed that was true.

"But why does she keep getting a UTI? I know she has had them in the past, but now it's become a regular thing," I asked

"Some of it has to do with aging. The other factor was that Abby has been on a steroid injection every three months for about a year to treat her skin allergies. Steroids lower the ability of her immune system to fight infection," Karen explained.

Hell, I knew this about steroids as I work in the pharmaceutical industry, but I had failed to connect the dots.

"This is like a Rubik's cube—solve one medical issue and create another," I commented.

"Yes, I would say that's the situation we have here. The important thing is to stop the UTIs, which will hopefully reduce or eliminate the seizures. Let's stop the steroids and give her more frequent, medicated baths for her skin condition. We'll give her pulsed antibiotic therapy to keep the UTIs and hopefully the seizures at bay," Karen recommended.

So that was the plan moving forward.

"Good thing I started purchasing pet insurance all those years ago when we adopted Bailey," I said to Alan. "I can't believe how the medical expenses are racking up with Abby alone. These antibiotics aren't cheap, and she will probably be on them indefinitely."

"This is like taking care of an old person. Their body starts to break down, and at thirteen, Abby is essentially a ninety-year-old person," Alan said.

It was difficult to think of Abby as this old. She was still in great shape and had a puppy-like disposition. I was grateful for that. She continued to get enjoyment from playing with her woobies, especially when we bought a new one. She looked forward to her daily walks and still followed us around the house to see what we were up to. We lived like this for a little while longer, enjoying each day with her as if it were a gift. Abby greeted every day the same way, too.

Months before, we had planned a two-week vacation in late June to Prince Edward Island (PEI), Canada. We had passed through there sixteen years

Last Dog

before during our road trip to Newfoundland with Bailey and had always regretted that we hadn't spend more time there. We'd decided to make it our summer vacation destination. We'd picked a house on the far eastern side of the island on Rollo Bay, which was actually more like a cove, an absolutely beautiful spot. With hundreds of miles of PEI coastline, Abby was sure to have a wet and wonderful time! We'd thought this would be appropriate since this might be her last road trip with us. Off we went, car packed to the rafters for the sixteen-hour ride ahead of us.

After a full day of driving with breaks to walk Abby, we made an overnight stop just over the border of Maine in a small town called Woodstock located in New Brunswick, Canada. We were excited for the next day as it was the last leg of our trip. It included a drive on a several-mile expanse on the extension bridge over the Gulf of Saint Lawrence.

Ah, what a view. As we approached the crest of the bridge, the island opened up before our eyes, laid out against the aquamarine water. We gave the car AC a break and rolled down the windows to feel the breeze and smell the salt water. Out my side view mirror, I saw Abby straining to get her nose up to the window opening for a good whiff. She just sat, taking in the view.

I turned and said to her, "Hey, sweetie, this is where you are going to live for the next two weeks!"

By the tone of my voice, Abby knew there was something to be excited about as I could hear her tail thumping against the back seat.

Once our wheels landed on the island, we were determined to reach the house by late afternoon. We drove non-stop. We didn't realize how large the island was and how far the house was located from Confederation Bridge. I think our anticipation also made our ultimate arrival seem all that much farther.

We were all a bit stiff getting out of the car after the long drive, but the sacrifice was worth it. We arrived at five p.m., and since the first day of summer was approaching and we were farther north, we had more hours of daylight.

Abby immediately started sniffing around, running toward the back of the house, which opened up to this great view of Rollo Bay. The house was set on a bluff overlooking the water. Unfortunately, it was too high and rocky for Abby to access it.

We had a special treat that evening. A full moon, but not just any full moon—a strawberry full moon. Indeed, it was tinted red as the name implies, making our arrival all the more special.

"You like this place, jelly bean," I asked as I petted the top of Abby's head. She just looked at me and panted excitedly. "Let's get you fed first so we can enjoy the rest of this evening in peace."

The first week on Prince Edward Island with Abby was great. Alan noticed immediately how well she was doing.

"She's got that old spring in her step," Alan remarked with a note of surprise.

"I know. It's so nice to see. It must be the excitement of being in a new place that is inspiring her," I offered.

Regardless of why, it was nice to have the "younger" Abby back with us, even just for a little while. Every one of our walks was along a shoreline

Last Dog

since the inner part of the island was ruled by mosquitoes and black flies that time of the year. Abby was fine with this since she could easily walk in and out of the Gulf of St Lawrence whenever she fancied, and she fancied it a lot.

But like elderly people, the good moments an old dog has can change in an instant, and they did for Abby. Once the second week of our vacation started, so did her seizures.

The first one happened in our car as we arrived at a beach we had traveled about a half-hour to get to. Luckily, the seizure was short-lived, and after a rest in the car with the AC on high, Abby sat up and seemed ready to get going. So we did. She was a little wobbly as she walked toward the shore but she made it and waded into the cool, calm gulf.

She was not totally back to herself so soon after the seizure. She looked a little confused, but the cool water seemed to soothe her. Then a small ripple of a wave ran over her head and down her nose, causing her to sneeze. Whether or not it was coincidental, soon after this episode, she developed a cough. Not the usual gagging sound she often made after sucking on her plush toys or the sound of kennel cough, either. Those sounds I know all too well.

So what would a vacation with Abby be without a visit to the veterinarian's office? We had done this on our first trip with her to Block Island almost eight years ago when she had gotten food poisoning from sneakily eating some foul fish remnants on the beach. She had been treating the shoreline like an all-you-can-eat buffet.

We had rushed back to the mainland on the first

ferry out the following morning, hiring a dog-friendly taxi to drive another hour to the local animal hospital. Abby had been fine after an IV and some medication.

When we were finished, she walked out of the recovery room with the usual pep in her step and a look that said, "Okay now what are going to do?" If she hadn't been so cute I would have strangled her. We had totally missed out on one of the few nice weather days we'd had that vacation on Block Island.

After a day of Abby coughing on this trip to PEI, we went to see the vet located just outside the town of Souris, where we were renting the house. Like everyone who met Abby, the vet's assistant and the vet fell in love with her. They couldn't get over how old she was given her puppy-like demeanor. It was moments like these that made us appreciate her all the more.

Unfortunately, the medication prescribed to help clear her lungs of the salt water caused her to have more frequent but short, seizure-like episodes called petit mals. These are usually very brief shaking episodes that can affect a dog while in motion or at rest. All of this took away the happy-go-lucky Abby we'd enjoyed during the first week of our vacation.

We had told the vet in Souris about Abby's history, including the seizures, and although he knew the risk, he thought prescribing the low dose would do no harm while helping clear her lungs, which was the priority at that moment.

Looking back on it, if I had only read all the potential side effects of the medication, I would have seen the seizure risk listed and not given it to her. We could have avoided all of this.

"This is what I am most concerned about, since the

Last Dog

water she inhaled puts her at risk for one of her lungs collapsing," the Souris vet explained. "The longer the salt water stays in her lungs, the more likely it will attract even more moisture, making the situation even worse."

Luckily, the half-life of the medication was relatively short, so once the drug left her system, the petit mals subsided. But poor Abby, this latest episode took a toll on her.

LEARNING: No matter how much or how little you understand about medications or the workings of the canine body, always thoroughly read information about the medication being recommended or prescribed for your dog.

Also, learn as much as you can about the medical condition and the implications it can have or what health risks it can cause.

Try to find out if there is a holistic alternative to the treatment being recommended. Holistic alternatives, while they don't come without risks, they can have fewer side effects, and in my limited experience, can be very effective.

In addition, tell your vet everything even if you don't think it is related; it just may be. Don't hesitate to ask questions or to challenge your vet or suggest something they have not considered.

WE MANAGED to finish out our vacation despite it all. Abby was a trooper. She took shorter walks, and we'd leave her at the house to nap while we'd go out for longer hikes.

Cynthia Flowers

It felt so odd to be without her, and to be without a dog on a hike, especially in this new and beautiful spot. The feeling was uncomfortable and almost disorienting.

The thought crossed my mind that this is what it would feel like if we were dog-free. Alan and I had made a pact a few years back that when the last of our dogs passed on, we would take a break from our long tenure and give ourselves the freedom to pursue some travel and a lifestyle that allowed for more spontaneity and more money, too. We would always talk about it as being a temporary, albeit different, phase in our lives.

But the feeling that washed over me during the Abby-less hike through the rolling sand dunes of Prince Edward Island told me that it wasn't going to be quite as we imagined.

When we returned home to the States, her coughing got less frequent but then resumed. After a week of this, we took Abby to our vet. Good thing we did, because Abby was given a more thorough examination. A chest x-ray showed her heart was so enlarged that it was crowding her lungs. Poor Abby had cardiovascular disease despite how physically fit she was!

It's speculation on my part, but I think the water inhalation incident was a tipping point that Abby's physical condition could not compensate for, because it had diminished her lung capacity. Her condition began to worsen, made evident by the fact that Abby was struggling to breathe while walking.

Just as in humans, for dogs an enlarged heart is usually a fatal prognosis. However, Abby was in good physical shape—at least she had that going for her. In addition, Karen started Abby on a low-dose antihypertensive to help dilate her arteries so her heart wouldn't have to work as hard. She also prescribed a diuretic to reduce the water buildup in her lungs.

Within two weeks, Abby was back to her old self and up for her daily walks, lasting longer and going farther. The wag in her tail was back as was her interest in the world around her. We knew her condition would eventually worsen even with the medications, but at least it would buy her some extra time to enjoy the rest of summer and perhaps through the end of the year.

 LEARNING: No matter how old your dog is, don't automatically attribute a change in their physical and/or mental status to aging. We did this with Abby when we noticed her slowing down shortly after Charlie passed away. This slow-down was noticeable rather quickly. I believe this change was the onset of her cardiovascular disease. If we had known about her condition earlier, we could have put her on medication sooner, which could have further improved the quality of her life.

Who knows, perhaps her seizures were linked to her enlarged heart. The literature is not conclusive on this connection, but there is enough to make me inclined to think there is one.

I WAS LUCKY to have enough vacation days plus the flexibility to work from home when needed, which allowed me to spend as much time as possible with Abby. Pessimistic about the chances of her making it to next summer, we made sure there was always someone home or arranged for our pet sitter, Erica, to take her for a walk every day. When I was home, I took the extra time to ride up to the Shawangunks so Abby could wade in the streams as the heat was getting more challenging for her to tolerate in her present condition.

The rest of that summer and early autumn were good days for Abby and us. Karen was happy with how she was responding to her medication. However, her seizures were still happening, and they were occurring more frequently, almost weekly.

"I think we should take her to a neurologist. I could kick myself. We should have done it when she first started having these seizures," I told Alan.

"It can't hurt," he agreed.

The neurologist did not seem alarmed. Given her age and seizure history, as well as the frequency and duration, he was confident that this was age-related.

"If it were caused by a tumor, it's probably a meningioma, a slow-growing tumor since these seizures started about three years ago. We would need to get an MRI to confirm, but I wouldn't recommend anesthesia for a dog her age. Besides, if we did find something, we can't do anything about it as surgery would not be an option for a dog her age," he explained.

I agreed, because I remembered how long it took Abby to get back her bearings after being under anesthesia last year for another procedure. Of course, we had the option of putting Abby back on anti-seizure medicine. But I explained Abby's poor experience on them and our reluctance to give it another try.

The neurologist understood and agreed, especially given that the dog in front of him was a happy pooch who didn't act like an old dog plagued by seizures and heart disease.

Last Dog

"At this age, it's all about giving her a good quality of life, so you need to weigh the pros and cons of medication accordingly," the neurologist shared, validating my feelings.

In late September, we took advantage of an offer made by a friend of Alan's to stay at his house in East Hampton, Long Island. We had been there before with Abby, and the calmness of Gardiner's Bay and the adjoining inlet provided her with enough swimming options. Abby kicked off the long weekend with a seizure while we were moving our luggage into the house. A friend of the person who lent us the house was there to meet us and witnessed it.

I saw the worried look on his face, and I reassured, "She will come out of the seizure soon, and there is nothing we can do but let her ride it out."

I think he was taken aback by my matter-of-fact tone. I can only imagine what he felt, because it wasn't that long ago when we had witnessed Abby's first seizure and had felt panic and helplessness overwhelm us. But despite it all, Abby managed to have a good time on that trip.

Abby met her fifteenth birthday head-on. We had Alan's family over for a Labor Day weekend barbeque. It doubled as a celebration of sorts for Abby with a bowl of vanilla ice cream that she lapped up posthaste!

I don't believe in jinxing oneself, but the timing of a conversation I had with a fellow dog owner a few weeks later about how well Abby was doing eerily coincided with what would be her last week with us.

She had been doing so well that week, and I had just gone back into the office after working from home for two days. I had taken her for a hike or two walks each day I was home. Abby had been in good spirits and full of energy. I was encouraged.

I had related this to my office colleagues, sharing that I had recently started Abby on bee pollen to help with her seasonal allergies. As an additional benefit, the pollen is believed to help support the immune system and promote energy.

Something that Friday pushed me to catch an earlier bus back to our home in upstate New York. I caught the four p.m. out of Port Authority. Just about twenty minutes into the ride while ironically I was looking through pictures of our dogs on my cell phone, it rang.

Erica, our dog sitter, pleaded, "I'm out, walking Abby on the rail trail, and she is having a seizure. What should I do?"

"She will come out of it in a few seconds. Just let her lay there until she gets up on her own. This may take a few minutes," I instructed.

Erica replied hesitantly, "Okay."

Erica called a few minutes later to give me an update.

"A passing cyclist stopped to help me get Abby into the car. I am heading back to your house and will stay with her until you get home," Erica said, somewhat relieved.

I was relieved, too, and not surprised that the episode ended as quickly as it did.

The bus I was on pulled into town a bit early, and I was thinking of making a quick stop at the store. Something made me dismiss the thought immediately, and I headed directly home. I'm glad I did. I walked into the living room to find Abby sitting on her bed.

Last Dog

She was sitting quietly, looking at Erica as she sat on the couch, talking to her in a reassuring way.

I knelt down on Abby's bed. "Hello, girly-girl, how is my sweetie doing?" I asked while scratching her favorite spot below her chin.

Then I felt her skin quiver, her body shake, and then her head shook, too. Another seizure embraced her as she lay on her side.

"It's okay, Abby," I whispered as I kept my hand on her for reassurance.

This one lasted longer than usual, and she was foaming at the mouth quite a bit. Then it seemed to end, and her breathing became rapid as expected. I exhaled hard. I think I had been holding my breath during Abby's seizure.

I stayed by her side, and Erica came over as we waited for the rapid breathing to slow. It did, but it was only a brief reprieve, because Abby was going into another seizure. This cycling right back into another seizure was something new, and it didn't stop.

"It's been at least twenty minutes since the first seizure when I came home. This has never happened before," I informed Erica.

After a failed attempt to get a pet ambulance to the house any time soon, we decided to get her into my car and take her to the animal emergency hospital.

But how were we to get Abby up and out of the house and into the car without accidentally dropping her? She wasn't in control of her movements and could violently flail while we carried her. The idea occurred to me to use the sheet on the dog bed as a stretcher to safely lift and carry her out to the car.

"I'm going to back the car up onto the lawn as

close to the front door as possible," I told Erica. She nodded in agreement.

Once I pulled up on the lawn, Erica and I and loaded Abby into the back hatch of my Honda CRV. She felt heavier than usual despite the rush of adrenaline pushing through my veins. Erica waved goodbye and yelled to let her know if I needed anything.

I raced down the driveway to take on my next challenge—getting Abby to the hospital fast enough to head off any cognitive damage this prolonged seizure episode might be causing.

LEARNING: *Status epilepticus* is an epileptic seizure lasting five minutes or longer. It consists of more than one seizure within a five-minute period without the individual returning to normal between them. *Status epilepticus* is a life-threatening medical emergency, particularly if treatment is delayed.

ERICA HAD CALLED the hospital to alert them I was on my way and to inform them of the nature of the emergency. I wove in and out of rush-hour traffic across the Mid-Hudson Bridge in the pelting rain almost instinctually. This was not the first time I had driven to this very same animal emergency hospital. Unfortunately, we had done this twice before with Charlie—the first time was when he was having an anaphylaxis reaction to what we guessed was a bee sting and then two years ago when he was having his last vestibular event.

I ran in, and instantly, the vet tech appeared, rolling

Last Dog

a stretcher to the car. I slowly opened the hatch, bracing my body against it to prevent Abby from falling out. She was not in an active seizure, but she was breathing rapidly and pretty much out of it. The poor girl had a muzzle full of foam, and she had defecated on herself during the ride. All I could think at this point was thankfully she wasn't aware of what was happening to her.

They rolled her into the back examination area, and after I gave them Abby's medical history and information about this latest event, they told me to go into one of the consultation rooms.

While I was waiting, I realized I hadn't called Alan back. I had quickly called him at the house when I realized what Abby was experiencing was something new. I was taken aback by Alan's casual response and relaxed tone on that first call. I later learned when I called him again that he had misunderstood and had just assumed it was one of Abby's regular seizure episodes.

When I explained the entire story, Alan realized the direness of the situation. I think I even told him the vet mentioned that we might need to put her to sleep.

The vet readily agreed with our wishes to give Abby time to see if treating her with Valium would break the cycle. Perhaps we could give her a chance to recover enough to assess any damage done to her cognitive and/or motor skills.

"I wouldn't go any longer than twenty-four to thirty-six hours to make a decision. At that point if the cycling doesn't cease, then there isn't really anything that can be done for her," the on-call vet cautioned.

With that last bit of news and Abby now sedated, I left her in the care of the hospital staff and returned home.

Going home, I drove more slowly, almost in a trance-like state. It was still raining, but the rush-hour traffic was gone. My body was recovering from the prolonged adrenaline rush, and I could feel the need for sleep creeping in. Luckily, I made it home before that feeling took hold.

But as soon as I got there, a foul aroma from the living room greeted me. I cleaned up the results of Abby having lost control of her bowels. I burned a few scented sticks to help rid the living room and adjacent den of the unpleasant smell and then made my way to bed. I fell asleep, hoping Abby would get through this.

Early Saturday morning, I awoke to a phone call from the animal emergency hospital. Abby had had a seizure in the early morning hours. They had administered Valium, and it seemed to bring it to a stop, we should come to see her that morning. Alan had finally returned home, and we made it to the hospital by late morning. Abby was awake, and she was in an upright laying position.

"This is the best Abby has been since you dropped her off last night," the vet said, trying to convey some hope.

Abby seemed unsure of her surroundings, but this was understandable since she was on Valium and had also been put on a sedative during the night to help her sleep. Alan and I spoke our usual doggie talk to her and knelt down in her closet-sized kennel to pet and reassure her. She then laid back down on her side to rest.

That was our only window of opportunity to see Abby conscious. I am so glad the timing was in our

Last Dog

favor for a change.

The vet was coming off her shift and wanted to know what our plan was for Abby. Since we were encouraged by what we had seen, we agreed to give Abby more time and to check on her in the morning.

On the ride home, Alan sounded more optimistic than I felt. He hadn't witnessed the violent seizures, and I was afraid there was significant brain damage that would threaten her recovery.

Erica called shortly after our return from the hospital and asked if it was okay for her to visit Abby either later that day or the next.

"Of course, and it's sweet of you to make the effort to see her," I thankfully replied. I told Erica about Abby's status, and she offered words of encouragement. But truthfully, we were all putting on a brave face.

Erica made it over to the animal hospital later that Saturday afternoon. She phoned me after her visit to say that despite Abby seeming out of it, Erica was glad she had gotten the chance to spend time with her.

Sometime after midnight, the new vet on shift called to say that Abby had had another seizure. She needed to know what we wanted to do.

"Get her through the night however you can, and we will be there in the morning," I adamantly replied.

Very early that morning, the vet tech called and suggested we get there sooner rather than later as Abby had been breathing rapidly for a while even though she was heavily sedated. Given her heart condition, they feared she might not last much longer. We raced back to the hospital while discussing what we would do next, but we didn't really come to a decision.

Cynthia Flowers

When we got there, another new vet was on shift. I am glad he was there, because he conveyed such compassion toward Abby and what we were going through.

He consulted with us about what had been going on with Abby since that morning and gave us an honest yet empathetic assessment of what our choices were.

He didn't hold out much hope for Abby's recovery. Given her age and confounding health issues, he was leaning toward the recommendation of putting her to sleep.

We agreed that was the likely decision, but we wanted to see her again before making it final. So we waited as they moved Abby by stretcher to the consultation room where we could have some privacy with her and our decision.

As they carried her into the room and placed the stretcher on the floor, Alan gasped. "I can't get over how small Abby looks. Such a difference from when we saw her yesterday. And when I saw her on Tuesday, she was fine."

I reminded him that she had been through a lot in these past two days. We both gently stroked her body and petted her behind the ears and below the neck, whispering her name in our usual way. Abby was oblivious. She lay on her side breathing rapidly with her eyes closed tight. Alan and I looked at each other. My eyes filled like saucers ready to spill over, and we decided together that the best thing for Abby was to let her go.

We called the vet back in and told him of our decision. He told us we could stay with her while he put her to sleep.

Last Dog

We were *never* offered that option when we brought Charlie here almost two years ago when he'd had his last vestibular event. The vet on shift at the time hadn't offered it, and we were so emotional that we didn't even think to ask.

Coincidentally, that vet was the first vet on shift when I had brought Abby in two days earlier. If there is a silver lining in all of this, it's that we did it right this time, and stayed by Abby's side until the end.

People can tell you about it, but their explanations fail to convey the sense of humanity and great loss you experience all at once. I sat on the floor next to her, gently stroking her coat. I half-wished the drugs would take effect quickly and half-wished that they wouldn't. I felt her life current pulse through her body. I didn't want it to end but knew it must. The rise of her breast slowed, and her breaths grew less frequent.

For a second, I felt a sense of peace. It almost seemed like she was just in a gentle sleep and no longer feeling discomfort. Then the time between breaths slowed even more…and then…stopped.

"There will be a few mechanical exhales as the body rids itself of the last bits of oxygen even though she is already gone," the vet gently explained.

Then, she was gone.

I continued to pet Abby after she passed. I leaned in closer to kiss her face for the last time, whispering to her, "Go see Charlie, my sweet girl."

Abby at Prince Edward Island.

Abby's 15th birthday.

Last Dog

Abby, napping at her foster home.

EPILOGUE

I named this book about our eighteen years of experience with dogs—starting with Jake and ending with Abby—*Last Dog*, because Abby truly reinforced how much we love dogs. Abby was a labor of love from beginning to end. She tried our patience, strained our wallets, and required the most training. Despite her age, we loved her youthful, unchecked exuberance at first. Then later in her life, we came to realize that even the healthiest of dogs require more support, patience, and understanding as they enter their "golden" years.

Everyone who knew Abby agreed that she required the most work of all of our dogs, but because she was such a sweetie, it more than made up for it. The closing line in the obituary I wrote for Abby, which I sent to all who knew her including her foster family, read: Good night, Sweet Abby.

I can't say when we will get another dog again. All I know is now is not the right time for us although we miss Abby and the others very much. Compared to our previous losses, the difference we experienced when Abby passed on was that it felt like we had lost Charlie, Bailey, and Ralf all over again.

Not only that, we miss the concept of caring for and being in the company of our dogs. I miss the sound of them lapping up water from their bowl, the sound of their bark, and the comical sounds Charlie made. All of

Last Dog

it. It just doesn't feel natural without them around.

I have a small, ceramic wall hanging that we keep near the kitchen sink where we'd prepare the dog food bowls. It reads: *A house is not a home without a dog.* A friend suggested now that Abby was gone that I should put it away. But I keep it there, because I still believe wholeheartedly in that sentiment. At some point, this house or another house of ours will be made a home again by a dog or two.

I hope my story is of help to first time or more experienced dog owners, guardians, caretakers, and dog lovers. Admittedly, we learned on the fly. Through the many trials and errors, we eventually created our own training schemes so our dogs were obedient enough to walk off-leash or to be let out in the backyard with little to no worry. We understood through observation what our dogs enjoyed doing most, and that was going for walks.

A dog's engagement with the world around them is intensified and is more satisfying when they go for a walk. I believe this keeps dogs young at heart and in mind and soul as they grow older. None of our dogs who made it to old age acted like an "old" dog. They still played with their toys, initiated play with us and each other, and never passed up an opportunity to go somewhere or to do something.

We found that there was an unspoken contract—as long as we gave them regular walks, we suffered very little in terms of behavioral issues. They were loyal and obedient and wanted to be around us as we were their pack leaders. And they had our love in return. I believe our dogs understood this.

Alan and I often joked that when our guys passed

over to the other side, they would be disappointed, because it might not be as good as they'd gotten with us! I hope that is true and *not* true, all at the same time.

BIBLIOGRAPHY

Arnold, Jennifer. *Through a Dog's Eyes*. New York: Spiegel & Grau, 2011.

Coren, Stanley. *How to Speak Dog: Mastering the Art of Dog—Human Communication.* Free Press, 2000.

Dutcher, Jim, and Jamie Dutcher. *The Hidden Life of Wolves.* The National Geographic Society, 2013.

Ellis, Shaun, and Monty Sloan. *Spirit of the Wolf*. Paragon Books, 2006.

Grambo, Rebecca L. *Wolf Legend Enemy Icon*. Firefly Books, 2005.

Grogan, John. *Marley & Me: Life and Love with the World's Worst Dog*. Harper Collins, 2005.

Holland, Jennifer S. *Unlikely Heroes: 37 Inspiring Stories of Courage and Heart from the Animal Kingdom*. Workman Publishing Company, 2014.

Horrowitz, Alexandra. *Inside of a Dog: What Dogs See, Smell, and Know*. Scribner, 2010.

Katz, Jon. *Talking to Animals: How You Can Understand Animals And They Can Understand You*. New York: Atria Books, 2017.

Masson Moussaieff, Jeffrey. *Dogs Never Lie About Love*: *Reflections on the Emotional World of Dogs*. Three Rivers, 1997

Millan, Cesar. Collection of books, television programs, and seminars.

Page, George. *Inside The Animal Mind*: *A Groundbreaking Exploration of Animal Intelligence*. Doubleday, 1999.

Rogers, Lesley J. *Minds of Their Own: Thinking and Awareness in Animals*. Westview Press, 1997.

Sheldrake, Rupert. *Dogs That Know When Their Owners Are Coming Home and Other Unexplained Powers of Animals*. Three Rivers Press, 1999.

Thomas Marshal, Elizabeth. *The Hidden Life of Dogs*. Pocket Books, 1993.

ABOUT THE AUTHOR

Cynthia Flowers is a strategist at a New York City advertising agency. She and her husband, Alan, reside part-time at their "sanctuary" in Upstate New York, where all of their dogs had enjoyed their lives. Early on in grade school writing class, Cynthia would often create stories where animals came to life as the main character. She enjoyed reading them aloud to her classmates, who looked forward to them, too.

Cynthia looks forward to sharing future adventures as she and her husband, Alan, embark on starting their dog hiking service. Hopefully, these future adventures will also include stories about a new dog of their own. Stay tuned.

Made in the USA
Lexington, KY
10 August 2018